THE WORLD'S
MOST SPECTACULAR
RAILWAY JOURNEYS

THE WORLD'S MOST SPECTACULAR **RAILWAY JOURNEYS**

50 of the most scenic, exciting, challenging
and exotic routes across the globe

Brian Solomon

with contributors:

Fred Matthews, Colin Nash, George Pitarys and Scott Snell

JOHN BEAUFOY PUBLISHING

CONTENTS

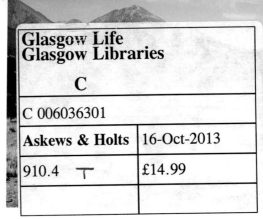

Half title page: The Furka Cogwheel Steam Railway.

Title page: The Swiss Alpine Narrow Gauge Matterhorn-Gotthard Bahn.

Above: The TranzAlpine, New Zealand.

INTRODUCTION

There is something undeniably compelling about a railway journey. The pleasure unfolds gradually – from the anticipation of entering a big city terminal, through the delights of watching the scenery roll by from the comfort and safety of a railway carriage to the thrill of gliding into a new destination. For the better part of two centuries, railway travel has provided passengers with the excitement of motion and speed through an ever-changing landscape. The story of railways began on Britain's Stockton & Darlington line in the 1820s, and this mode of transport proved so successful that it soon spread around the world. Where the earliest lines were built with billiard-table grades, ultimately engineers learned clever ways to allow railways to traverse just about every conceivable terrain. Today lines climb to the tops of towering peaks, run through rugged river valleys, and even pass below major bodies of water. Early railways stunned travellers when their locomotives managed to puff along at 'high speeds' of 20 to 30 mph (32 to 48 km/h); today some trains are regularly scheduled at more than 200 mph (322 km/h).

Each of the journeys selected is spectacular for its own significant reasons. Some feature stunning scenery, others exemplify clever engineering – long tunnels, precipitous ascents and massive urban terminals – while others are fascinating because of sustained high-speed running. Journeys like those of Canada's *Rocky Mountaineer*, Conway Scenic's passage through Crawford Notch and Germany's Zugspitzbahn are operated for the benefit of tourists wanting to experience the natural splendour of the regions they serve; others, including the *Eurostar*, Japanese *Shinkansen* and California's *Capitols*, are operated as part of a transportation network with the primary purpose of moving people as efficiently and comfortably as possible to many destinations. The freedom to get on and off trains at will remains one of the great benefits and joys of railway travel. While some journeys require advance planning and specific tickets for individual trains, others, such as many in Europe, can be enjoyed by making spontaneous decisions to board trains, or equally to get off them with little notice to explore destinations encountered en route.

Readers may be familiar with some of the journeys included in the book, but we hope that many of the other journeys profiled will cover new ground, and thereby open readers' eyes to the beauties of horizons previously unexplored.

Brian Solomon

Opposite: The Canadian scenery on the Rocky Mountaineer's 'Whistler Sea to Sky Climb' train is spectacular from its start at Vancouver to its finish at Whistler as it travels up Howe Sound and through British Columbia's coast range mountains. Here, the train is skirting Porteau Cove only 30 miles (48 km) from the terminal at Vancouver.

PACIFIC SURFLINER

Amtrak's Coastal Corridor

Brian Solomon

Originally the *San Diegan* route and today known as Amtrak's *Pacific Surfliner*, this is a highly scenic route that thrives as Amtrak's second most patronized intercity service (after the Northeast Corridor). Unlike most Amtrak long-distance services which use equipment from a general pool and are not 'train-specific', *Pacific Surfliner* trains use distinctively styled double-deck equipment, lettered for the service and painted in shades of blue and aqua to resemble the deep blue Pacific Ocean. *Pacific Surfliners* operate over the former Santa Fe Railway line between San Diego and Los Angeles, with some services continuing on former Southern Pacific lines to Santa Barbara and San Luis Obispo (on the route also served by the *Coast Starlight*). The San Diego–LA section is the busiest with 15 round trips weekdays.

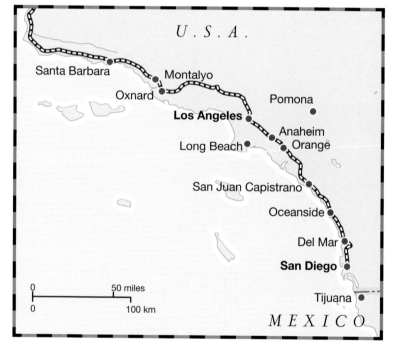

The best place to board the *Pacific Surfliner* is at the historic Los Angeles Union Passenger Terminal (now officially 'Los Angeles Union Station'). This 1939-built architectural gem, featured in countless Hollywood films and television programmes over the years, was designed by LA architects John and Donald Parkinson. The station combines a blend of Spanish and Moorish motifs in a classic art deco style. It was the last of the great American big city terminals completed – originally served by Southern Pacific, Union Pacific and Santa Fe. Today, it is a multi-modal transportation hub where passengers can connect from Amtrak and Metro-Link suburban stations to local LA transit, including light rail and subway lines.

From the window of the train you'll find an unending mix of sea birds, breaching dolphins, skilled ocean-surfers, pleasure boats, container ships, while enjoying the sight of pelicans gliding along the coast. To get the best view, it is

important to select the ocean side of the train when boarding; since LAUPT is a stub end terminal, this takes forethought and varies depending on whether you are travelling northward towards Santa Barbara or southward towards San Diego. When departing LAUPT you want to be on the left-hand side of the train northbound, but on the right-hand side when southbound.

Heading towards San Diego, the *Pacific Surfliner* navigates urban Los Angeles, undoubtedly familiar because of the numerous films made here over the years; passengers will probably feel a sense of déjà vu when they see the channelled LA River, the setting for numerous high-speed movie chase scenes. East of LA, *Pacific Surfliner* stops at the classic Santa Fe station in Fullerton, before negotiating a junction for the southward trip along the coast. The train finally reaches the coast near San Juan Capistrano, famous for its old Spanish Mission and the flocks of sparrows that return en masse every 23 October.

Running along the coast, the train passes San Clemente. At Oceanside, the tracks meander inland but the station offers multi-modal connections to a variety of destinations. No less than four different railway services connect here, including the Sprinter which uses frequent lightweight European trains to reach Escondido. Below Oceanside, the line hugs cliff sides at Del Mar, where flocks of coasting pelicans glide alongside the train.

Above: A streamlined Electro-Motive F59PHI diesel works the Pacific Surfliner on its coastal journey from LAUPT to San Diego. The locomotive was styled and profiled to blend with the California cars it hauls.

At both San Diego's historic mission-styled Santa Fe station and at Old Town, *Pacific Surfliner* connects with the famous San Diego Trolley that provides a modern transit connection across the San Diego metro-area, and reaching right to the Mexican border at Tijuana.

The serene coastal splendour of the aptly-named *Pacific Surfliner* offers virtually a sea-voyage by rail. Take the trip towards dusk and watch the sun set into the deep blue of the Pacific from the comfort of your seat!

Opposite: Amtrak Pacific Surfliner *rolls along San Clemente beach. More than ten daily round trips between LA and San Diego offer passengers both convenience and comfort.*

Left: Opened in 1939, Los Angeles Union Passenger Terminal was frequented by movie stars in its heyday. After decades of gradual decline, it was restored and revived during the 1990s and now serves more trains than ever before, among them Amtrak's Pacific Surfliner.

Opposite: Amtrak's Pacific Surfliner *is one of its few distinctively painted trains; its colours are designed to mimic the hues of the Pacific on a sunny day. A San Diego-bound train passes San Clemente Pier.*

CAPITOL CORRIDOR

Sacramento to San Jose on the old SP

Brian Solomon

Amtrak's *Capitol Corridor* connects Sacramento and San Jose – so named in recognition of California's current and historic capital cities. The trains on the route are called *Capitols* and operate with the modern double-deck *California Cars* specifically designed for medium-distance California runs. Historically, the Sacramento–Martinez–Oakland route was among the busiest passenger lines on the old Southern Pacific system; however, in the 1950s the service was downgraded, leaving only long-distance runs by the coming of Amtrak in May 1971. This situation was reversed in 1990 when a popular bond issue was passed allowing California to redevelop passenger rail corridors. The first new trains to operate with this public mandate were three round trips on the *Capitols* route.

Over the last two decades substantial infrastructure investment has improved the service and many more trains were added to the run. Unlike many American routes that see only one daily long-distance train, the *Capitols* route operates as many as 16 round trips most weekdays. Although the line connects the densely populated cites at both ends of its line, the route is extraordinarily scenic, and like California's *Pacific Surfliner* route is among the most scenic intercity lines in the United States. The frequency of service, combined with excellent public transit and long-distance rail connections, has made the *Capitols* an extraordinary transportation success. This is especially remarkable for California, the first American state to fully embrace the 20th-century highway culture.

While the *Capitol Corridor* connects Sacramento and San Jose, the range of individual services vary, with the greatest number of trains working between Oakland and Sacramento. Furthermore, one train originates east of Sacramento in the Sierra foothills at Auburn. Sacramento Station is a well-connected

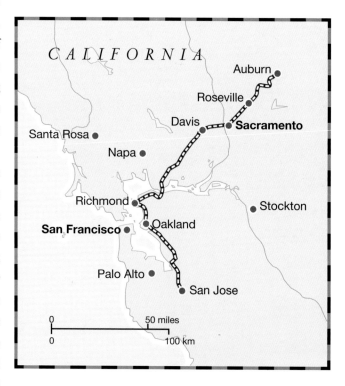

Opposite: The afternoon sun catches an Amtrak Capitols train as it follows the shore of San Pablo Bay at Pinole, California. Much of the run from Fairfield to Richmond, California hugs inland waterways.

Above: Amtrak's Capitols use Union Pacific's former Southern Pacific line along the Carquinez Straits. A westward Capitols train skirts the shore near Martinez, California.

intermodal hub, where passengers are afforded rail connection with the Regional Transit District light rail system. Just a short walk from the station will be found the city's premier tourist attraction: the California State Railroad Museum, which houses one of the most significant historic railroad collections in North America. This is worth a visit; among the displays are historic locomotives including: *4-4-0 Governor Stanford*, named for influential Leland Stanford, a noted California businessman, railroad empire builder and politician; Southern Pacific's last built and only surviving 'Cab Ahead' steam locomotive, a type specifically designed by Baldwin for SP's Donner Pass crossing; and a variety of historic diesels, including a former Western Pacific F7A, similar to that once used on the *California Zephyr* domeliner.

Leaving Sacramento, *Capitols* trains cross the Sacramento River on the famed I-Street Bridge drawbridge with tracks on the lower level and the street above. Soon after passing West Sacramento, the line crosses the 'Yolo Bypass' flood control area on a series of fills and trestles. Interstate 80 freeway runs parallel on the left side of the tracks. Davis is an important station stop. This is a railroad junction with California Northern's former SP West Valley Line – once an important passenger route for trains to Oregon, today this route is strictly used for local freight. A preserved signal tower and the railroad station were both built in a Spanish Revival style, and are located within the 'wye' that allows trains to access the California Northern. As the location of a large University of California campus, Davis station is heavily used by students travelling to and from the Bay Area.

West of Davis the railroad crosses the broad level expanse of the largely agricultural Central valley. Near Vacaville, the line passes near Travis Air Force Base, where it is common to see C5A Galaxy military transports and other large aircraft circling the tarmac. A station stop is made at Fairfield, and beyond is another railroad junction with a California Northern branch line. To the west the line skirts Suisun Bay, a tidal estuary that comprises part of the inland waterway that ultimately feeds the Pacific at the Golden Gate. Stored ships can seen to the left as the line approaches Bahia, after which the railway passes an industrial area and then crosses the massive Suisun Bay Bridge – the largest double-track railway bridge west of the Mississippi River. Prior to its completion by SP in 1930, entire trains were ferried across the Carquinez Straits between Benicia and Port Costa. Although enormous, the railway bridge is flanked by two even larger highway spans that carry the intensely travelled Interstate 680 highway which is the railroad's primary competitor for intercity traffic.

After a station stop at Martinez, where passengers can change for *San Joaquin* trains destined for Bakersfield, the line passes a small Union Pacific freight yard at Ozol, then hugs the south shore of the Carquinez Straits which flows into San

Left: Between the stations at Emeryville and Jack London Square, the line passes the Port of Oakland, California, which serves as a major North American container port. Beyond the Port are the approach spans to the San Francisco–Oakland Bay Bridge.

Below: The double-deck California Cars were specifically designed for California intercity Amtrak services. This is the interior view of the upper deck of a lounge car.

Pablo Bay. The best views are available from the right-hand side of the train. At Crockett the line passes below the spans of Interstate 80, with four lanes in each direction that are clogged with traffic day and night. A station stop at Richmond allows passengers to change to electric trains operated by Bay Area Rapid Transit (known universally as BART) which runs via Oakland to San Francisco and beyond. Additional Bay Area stops are made at Berkeley (location of another important UC campus), and Emeryville (where a bus connection is made for San Francisco). At the port of Oakland the line skirts the massive international shipping terminus. To reach the Oakland Station at Jack London Square, the railway transits city streets where it shares space with road vehicles and pedestrians. Beyond Oakland, the line passes through industrial and densely populated communities in the East Bay, making stops at Hayward and at Fremont-Centerville. To reach San Jose, tracks cross the Don Edwards wildlife preserve at Alviso where a host of birds can be seen.

A stop is made at Santa Clara, and the route terminates at San Jose's Cahill Street Station. At both these points, connections are available with Cal-Train (which runs north to San Francisco) and the Altamont Commuter Express which runs at rush-hours to Stockton via Altamont Pass. In addition, Santa Clara Valley Transportation Authority light rail makes connections at San Jose.

Above: Amtrak uses the old Southern Pacific station at Davis, California. This classic Spanish Revival-style building once served trains on both the California Pacific route mainline and SP's West Valley Line. Today it is used by Capitols trains as well as California Zephyr and Coast Starlight.

AMTRAK'S COAST STARLIGHT

Seattle to Los Angeles

Brian Solomon

The *Coast Starlight* is one of Amtrak's most popular long-distance trains. Connecting Seattle and Los Angeles, it spans most of the distance between the Canadian and Mexican frontiers. The core of the journey runs on former Southern Pacific lines, while the section between San Jose and LA covers much of the route of SP's famous *Daylight*. The classic streamlined *Daylight* began service in the 1930s, and for a few years in the 1940s SP operated a companion train called the *Starlight* that was known for its party atmosphere. Amtrak assumed intercity operations from SP and other railroads in 1971, and the concept for a through Seattle–LA run was a result of Amtrak's coordinated strategy.

The *Coast Starlight*, along with most other Amtrak long-distance services west of Chicago, uses standard Superliner cars which offer a high-level double-deck design. Most passengers ride on the top level. Especially popular is the Sightseer lounge with its glass roof that allows for exceptional views of the passing scenery. It is the next best thing to SP's full-length dome cars made famous by the *Shasta Daylight* train in the 1950s and 1960s.

Just before midday, the daily *Coast Starlight* begins its southward journey in Seattle. On the 187-mile (300-km) trip between Seattle, Washington and Portland, Oregon the train operates over Burlington Northern Santa Fe's line. Then for the remainder of the journey south from Portland, the train works Union Pacific's former SP lines. South of Eugene, the *Coast Starlight* ascends Pengra Pass in the Oregon Cascades, where the line hooks through a series of horseshoe curves, and passes tunnels and snow sheds on its way to Cascade Summit. This was among the last major mainline routes completed in the United States, and was opened in the 1920s to supplant SP's original Oregon route over the sinuous Siskiyou Line. While the

Opposite: A trip on the Coast Starlight features many miles of oceanside running. The train sails across the steel tower-supported viaduct at Gaviota, California near Santa Barbara.

Coast Starlight crosses the Cascades in darkness when travelling southward (except in the height of summer), a daylight trip over this amazing mountain pass can be enjoyed by taking the northward train. Incidentally, Southern Pacific didn't acknowledge 'north' and 'south' in its timetable, and historically all trains were either eastbound or westbound, with eastbound trains heading away from its headquarters in San Francisco, and westbound running towards San Francisco, regardless of actual compass direction. Confused? Riding the southward *Starlight* you are going 'railroad west' until you reach Oakland, California, and from there you are travelling 'railroad east'.

Overnight the southward train passes the immense volcanic cone of Mt Shasta, as it drops down the grade to the traditional railroad town of Dunsmuir, California, located near the top of the Sacramento River valley. Between Redding and Sacramento, and beyond to Fairfield, the line passes through the broad and fertile expanse of California's agricultural Central valley. While between Roseville (in the northern Sacramento suburbs)

Above: Amtrak's Coast Starlight serves the modern station at Oakland's Jack London Square that was built in the mid-1990s to replace the old Southern Pacific-era station at 16th Street that was damaged in the Loma Prieta earthquake of October 1989.

and Oakland, California the *Starlight* shares its route with both the *California Zephyr* and *Capitols* trains. Scenic highlights of this run are coastal views along the Carquinez Straits and San Pablo Bay. To get the best views for the remainder of the journey, the wise traveller should select a seat on the right-hand side of the train at this stage of the trip. At Oakland's Jack London Square, the train navigates street trackage and makes its station stop just a short walk away from shops and a ferry terminal (with regular service to the San Francisco waterfront).

At San Jose, connections are available to Cal-Train's peninsula 'commutes' to San Francisco. Although once part of the sprint for SP's *Daylight*, there have been no through long-distance services to San Francisco since 1971. Beyond the sprawling San Jose suburbs, the *Starlight* pauses at America's garlic capital, Gilroy. The line swings sharply to the west at Sargent, and navigates the narrow confines of Chittenden Pass to reach the agricultural centre at Watsonville Junction. The line then resumes a southward course and passes through the Elkhorn Slough wildlife refuge offering a view of multitudes of sea birds. After a brief station stop in Salinas, the train continues through the agricultural Salinas valley where vegetables are grown for consumption across America.

The engineering highlight of this portion of the trip is the descent of Cuesta Grade, otherwise known as Santa Margarita Hill. Here the railway passes through a series of tunnels and navigates several sweeping horseshoe curves as it winds down the Coast Range to San Luis Obispo. On a clear day, passengers will get amazing elevated views of the Pacific beyond the mountains. In steam days, passenger trains ascending Cuesta regularly required helpers. South of San Luis Obispo, the line climbs Casmalia Hill, and passes through the Vandenberg Air Force Base as it hugs the Pacific coast for many miles.

The azure expanse of the ocean is as captivating today as it was for passengers on SP's luxury limiteds generations ago. Many of these Pacific views are only to be appreciated from the train, since much of the coast line here is inaccessible to the public. The line continues to Santa Barbara and then, after more oceanside running, it passes the sprawling LA suburbs. It terminates after sunset at Los Angeles Union Passenger Terminal – an art deco gem and one of the west's greatest railway stations.

Below: Amtrak's Seattle-bound Coast Starlight *descends the Cascades near Field, Oregon. This sinuous mountain crossing is among the route's many scenic highlights. SP completed the line in the late 1920s, putting it among the last major railway lines finished in the West.*

CALIFORNIA ZEPHYR

Across the Plains, over the Rockies, Sierra, and Beyond!

Brian Solomon

The launch of the classic *California Zephyr* in 1949 was a joint effort between Burlington, Rio Grande, and Western Pacific to connect Chicago and the California Bay Area. The train itself was an expansion of Burlington's popular streamlined *Zephyr* trains which since the mid-1930s had connected key midwestern cities. Using Budd-built, shot-welded, stainless-steel cars hauled by General Motors' diesel-electrics, these trains helped to define a new era of rail passenger travel in North America. The *California Zephyr* combined the very finest Budd-built train with a truly spectacular transcontinental crossing. Multiple elevated glass-topped Vista Domes and a round-end dome-observation tail car allowed passengers some of the finest views in the west. Despite its popularity with travellers, by the 1960s the train was unprofitable. The financially weak Western Pacific was unable to sustain its portion of the trip and in April 1970 the train was discontinued. Sadly, this was only little more than a year before

Opposite: Working west in the Truckee River Canyon, the train is two nights west of Chicago, and passing through its last mountain range – California's Sierra Nevada – before reaching the Pacific Coast. Where the classic California Zephyr (1949–70) used the Western Pacific route through the Feather River Canyon, Amtrak's train takes the Donner Pass crossing.

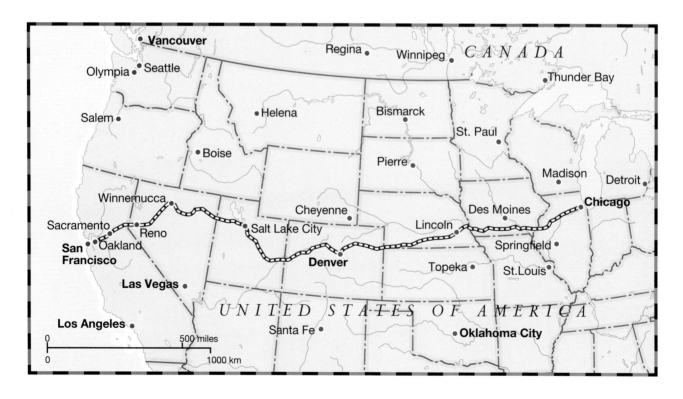

Congress created Amtrak to take over operations of America's national intercity passenger trains from the private railroads. Rio Grande initially refrained from Amtrak operation and continued to operate its Denver–Salt Lake City portion of the *California Zephyr* route until 1983.

Today Amtrak's *California Zephyr* follows much of the route used by the historic 1950s domeliner, yet features a few notable deviations, and uses *Superliner* equipment instead of the classic Budd cars. Travelling west, Amtrak's *CZ* begins its journey at Chicago Union station, Amtrak's midwestern hub, a principal terminus for trains serving cities around the country. Today's uses the historic Burlington Route west of Chicago, traversing the busy 'Triple-Track' mainline via La Grange and Aurora, Illinois, where tracks are shared with a steady parade of Metra suburban trains, as well as BNSF freights. The *Zephyr* is often routed on the middle track to overtake the all-stops Metra trains.

La Grange was home to General Motors' Electro-Motive Division that constructed most American diesel-electric locomotives from the late 1930s to the early 1990s (at which time GM shifted production to Canada). In GM's pioneering diesel days, Burlington was among its most loyal customers, and many of the early diesels raced up and down Burlington's lines on break-in runs. West of Aurora the mainlines divide, and the *CZ* takes the line to Galesburg – an important

Above: Among the most spectacular vistas on the Zephyr route is that from the rim of the American River Canyon on Donner's west slope. Here the tracks ride a shelf 2,000 feet (600 m) above river level. In steam days, Southern Pacific stopped some trains here, where wooden viewing platforms allowed passengers to take in the view.

freight hub where former Santa Fe and Burlington lines converge. The journey to Denver across the plains is largely accomplished overnight.

Although Denver Union was once a region passenger hub, today the *CZ* is the only daily passenger train to call here. Having used BNSF lines from Chicago to Denver, west of Denver *CZ* follows former Rio Grande's Denver & Salt Lake route, a line now operated by Union Pacific. The railroad climbs sharply as it ascends the Colorado Front Range, and navigates the tortuous 'Big Ten Curves' giving passengers a clear view across the plains. The skyscrapers of Denver dot the near horizon while the great expanse beyond hints at the great distance the train has travelled from Chicago. On its way up the Front Range, *CZ* passes through a number of short tunnels, before reaching the great Moffat Tunnel. Opened to rail traffic in 1928, Moffat Tunnel was part of a line relocation that replaced the old 'Giant's Ladder' – an exceptionally sinuous crossing of the Front Range that was one of the highest railways ever built in the United States. The tunnel is 6.2 miles (10 km) long, and crests the Continental Divide at 9,239 feet (2,816 m) above sea level. Tracks exit the confines of the mountain at the popular ski resort of Winter Park, a station stop for the *CZ*. Continuing west, passengers can revel in a host of memorable mountain vistas. Especially breathtaking are views in Gore Canyon, and beyond in the confines of Glenwood Canyon. Stops are made at

Above: Amtrak's California Zephyr rolls west on the rails of the old Denver & Rio Grande Western (now operated by Union Pacific) through Gore Canyon, Colorado. At the back of the train is privately owned, former Lehigh Valley observation car 353.

Glenwood Springs, and Grand Junction, after that the journey is largely nocturnal as the train runs across the Utah Desert, over Soldier Summit, to Salt Lake City.

The *Zephyr* meets the rising sun somewhere across the wide expanse of the Nevada Desert. Between Alazon (west of Wells, Nevada) and Winnemucca, the train uses the old 'Paired Track' that consists of parallel single-track mainlines. Today both routes are operated by Union Pacific, but historically one line belonged to Southern Pacific and the other to Western Pacific (absorbed by UP in 1981 and 1996 respectively). At Winnemucca, the Amtrak's *CZ* deviates from the historic route. The old Domeliner took Western Pacific's line across the Black Rock and Smoke Creek deserts via Sand Pass, and then through the spectacularly scenic Feather River Canyon – a route now exclusively a freight line, and beyond via Sacramento, Stockton and Altamont Pass. Instead, Amtrak's *CZ* follows SP's Overland Route, once the line made famous by the *Overland Limited* and *City of San Francisco*, choice runs of great railway writer Lucius Beebe who travelled widely by train in the mid-20th century. Between Winnemucca and Reno, the old SP line hugs the barren desert floor. Reno is a famed gambling centre and high-rise casinos are visible from the train.

Above: The westward California Zephyr catches the fading light of the setting sun as it ascends the east slope of California's Donner Pass. Soon the train will be over the summit and drifting down through the tall conifers that dot the west slope heading towards the lights of Sacramento.

West of Reno, the line begins the famous ascent of Donner Pass –named for the doomed pioneer settlers, the Donner party, who were trapped in the mountains by an early heavy snowfall. Many of them died. The best time to travel over Donner is in mid- to late winter when snowfall on the pass is measured in feet rather than inches. Here, Amtrak's *CZ* offers vistas not easily afforded to casual travellers by any other means. As it climbs, the railroad crosses the state-line into California as it negotiates the sinuous Truckee River Canyon – shared with Interstate 80 and a freshwater flume. The narrow confines of the canyon and difficult grade resulted in eastward and westward tracks being constructed on separate, but parallel, alignments. At several places tracks come together, only to separate again on their way up to the summit of the Sierra. Amtrak serves a station in the trendy mountain town of Truckee.

West of here the line loops through Cold Stream Canyon, where it makes a sharp horseshoe to maintain a steady gradient to the summit. At Andover, upon passing a short tunnel, the line runs along a narrow shelf high above the crystalline blue waters of Donner Lake (to the right of the tracks). Climbing on the far side

is Interstate 80. In the past the railroad clung to the cliffside around the north face of Mt Judah using a series of snow sheds and short tunnels. Sadly, this spectacular crossing of Donner Pass was abandoned in 1993 in favour of the 1920s line that goes directly beneath the mountain through a tunnel nearly 2 miles (3.2 km) long.

The line crests Donner Summit near Norden, California, today the location of a ski resort and a passing siding where Amtrak routinely either meets or overtakes a freight train. From Norden the railway descends the long grade towards Sacramento. Only the short uphill section in Long Ravine near Colfax, California keeps Donner from holding the record as America's longest unbroken mountain climb. Spectacular views abound on both sides of the tracks. Between Roseville and Oakland, the *CZ* shares the route of the *Coast Starlight* and *Capitols* trains, which is especially scenic west of Fairfield and along San Pablo Bay. The *CZ* terminates at Emeryville, across the bay from San Francisco. Historically passengers arrived in San Francisco by means of a short ferry trip from the Oakland Mole; today bus transfers are the normal option. Even passengers of the historic trains were unable to arrive in San Francisco by rail from the east. Yet, the beckoning lights of America's Emerald City is a fine conclusion to a great transcontinental journey.

Below: Amtrak's eastward California Zephyr *climbs at Crystal Lake, California. The building of the railroad in the 1860s resulted in deforestation around Donner Pass as timber was needed for the tracks and extensive snow sheds. Erosion of the top soil has prevented significant re-growth.*

AMTRAK'S EMPIRE BUILDER

James J. Hill's Transcon

Brian Solomon

In the 1890s, James J. Hill built his Great Northern transcontinental route from the Twin Cities of Minneapolis-St. Paul, Minnesota, across North Dakota, the northern tier of Montana, the Idaho panhandle, and over the Washington Cascades to the Puget Sound port at Seattle. Unlike the earlier transcon lines that largely funded construction with extensive federal land-grants and cash subsidy, Hill's Great Northern was primarily funded with private capital. Hill's sound business sense led him to construct branches to ensure that adequate traffic developed along his lines. His forethought paid off, and he was among the most successful railroad moguls of his day. His success enabled him to control not only his connections, but one of his chief rivals as well, earning him the reputation as the 'Empire Builder'. After Hill died in 1916, Great Northern introduced a new classy flagship train named in his honour called the *Empire Builder*. This train survived as one of America's finest long-distance limiteds until the advent

Opposite: On a warm July morning, having crested the Continental Divide at Marias Pass, Amtrak's eastward Empire Builder glides downgrade at Grizzly, Montana. The peaks in the distance are in Glacier National Park. The location is named for the large carnivores that can occasionally be seen trackside.

of Amtrak in 1971. Today it remains one of Amtrak's most popular trains; using Superliner bi-level cars it connects Chicago with the Pacific Northwest over most of its historic route.

The train begins at Chicago Union Station, and today uses Canadian Pacific's former Milwaukee Road route via Wisconsin to the Twin Cities, instead of the historic route via Burlington's line along the Mississippi River. West from the Twin Cities, the train follows the historic Great Northern, a route now owned and operated by GN successor, Burlington Northern Santa Fe – one of the largest freight railways in the United States.

Below: Amtrak's eastward Empire Builder approaches Browning, Montana on the former Great Northern mainline. As one of the principal northern transcontinental routes, the old GN is a heavily travelled freight line as well as an Amtrak route.

In north-central Montana, the *Empire Builder* crosses Marias Pass that runs at the edge of Glacier National Park. At Marias Summit a larger-than-life statue of John Stevens stands to mark this great man who in the 1890s surveyed the Great Northern route for Hill, including this low crossing of the Rockies. Wildlife from the park occasionally makes it trackside; keep an eye out for bearded Rocky Mountain goats – the symbol of Great Northern – as well as grizzly bears. On the west slope of Marias, at Essex, Montana the train will pause at the famous Izaac Walton Inn, one of several 'flag stops' along the line. This popular mountain inn is a favourite with railway enthusiasts. Whitefish, Montana, located at the base of the pass, is the next station, featuring classic building dating from Great Northern days.

In Washington State, the line crosses Stevens Pass, named for John Stevens, where the line uses the famous Cascade Tunnel, the longest railroad tunnel in the USA. This present routing is the third, and lowest, railroad crossing of Stevens Pass. Earlier crossings were fraught with difficulties, especially the risk of avalanches. On the final leg of the transcontinental run, the *Empire Builder* skirts Puget Sound, stopping at Everett, and Edmonds Washington before reaching its terminus at Seattle.

HUDSON RIVER VALLEY

New York City to Albany

Brian Solomon

One of the great transportation moguls of the 19th century was Cornelius 'Commodore' Vanderbilt (1794–1877), who having earned a fortune with steamboats, shifted his focus to railroading in the 1860s. Using the New York & Harlem and New York & Hudson River Railroads as his foundation, he acquired the New York Central and blended these key properties together as the New York Central System. By the time he died in 1877, the New York Central System connected New York, Chicago and St. Louis and represented one of the great transportation networks of the railroad age. New York Central's lines were famous for their low-grade route characterized by riverside running, and became commonly known as the 'Water Level Route' – a description that implies efficiency as well as scenic splendour.

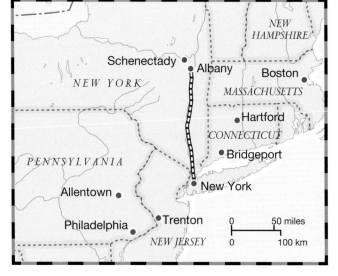

From its famed Grand Central Terminal, New York Central operated a host of well-known trains, including its flagship *Twentieth Century Limited* – an exclusive 'extra-fare' all-Pullman sleeper express train to Chicago that spared no expense nor made unnecessary stops. In its day, it was the conveyance of the rich and powerful, offering the finest and fastest means of travel between New York and Chicago.

New York Central and its famed flagship disappeared in the late 1960s, but its Water Level Route survives as a primary corridor and hosts a variety of long-distance trains. Amtrak's trains leave from New York's Pennsylvania Station on 34th street, which lacks the classic glamour of Grand Central, but offers better connections with Amtrak's other regional services. For those wishing to depart from Grand Central, suburban operator Metro-North operates commuter trains as far north as Poughkeepsie, and a change of trains can be made there for points further out.

Amtrak operates a host of trains along the Hudson River Route to Albany and beyond; Empire Service trains run frequently to Albany and Schenectady, with

some services continuing beyond to Buffalo and Niagara Falls. The daily *Maple Leaf* offers a cross-border service to Toronto, while its *Adirondack* serves Montreal, and its *Ethan Allen* runs to Rutland, Vermont. However, the most comfortable means of travel is on the *Lake Shore Limited* that runs the length of the Water Level Route to Chicago and carries Viewliner sleeping cars and a diner. While coach seats are comfortable, the wise traveller will book a compartment in the Viewliner. Be sure to request accommodation on the left-hand side of the train, as the finest scenery is on the Hudson River side. The *Lake Shore Limited* departs Penn Station in the afternoon, an ideal time to take in the splendour of the lower Hudson valley. The first few miles are on former New York Central's West Side Line, a route largely used by freight until converted to the role of a Penn Station link 20 years ago. After passing beneath Othmar Ammann's magnificent trans-Hudson George Washington Bridge, the line crosses the Harlem River and joins the Grand Central Route at Spuyten Duyvil. The Henry Hudson Parkway – named for the Dutch-sponsored English explorer who navigated the river that also bears his name – is to the right of the train and crosses the Harlem on a tall arched bridge parallel to Amtrak's route.

Near Tarrytown, the line passes below the massive Tappen Zee Bridge that carries the New York Thruway across the Hudson. Trains serving New York City

Above: One of Amtrak's General Electric-built dual-mode Genesis diesel-electric/electric locomotives roars northward along the Hudson near Scarborough. In the distance is the New York State Thruway's famed Tappan Zee Bridge which spans the river at one of its widest points.

are required to operate electrically. Amtrak and Metro-North both operate fleets of 'dual-mode' locomotives that work off high-voltage third-rail in the city terminals, and then switch to diesel-electric operation once in the open air beyond city tunnels. Third-rail continues all the way to Croton-Harmon to support an all-electric intensive suburban service. Beyond the electrified zone is the finest scenery. The river narrows near Peekskill – named for Dutch mariner Jan Peek; originally 'Peek's Kill' ('kill' meaning creek or estuary) – and the railway makes a sharp turn through the station. Sharp eyes will pick up the right-of-way of another railway on the far side of the Hudson. This is the old New York, West Shore & Buffalo, a one-time competitor to New York Central, later integrated into the New York Central System. While devoid of passenger services for more than 50 years, this remains a heavy freight route south of Albany. Watch for long container trains winding along on the far shore.

North of Peekskill, the line crosses a long fill at Roa Hook, and then at Anthony's Nose the Hudson narrows further and, opposite Iona Island, the line hugs a rock wall and cuts through a short tunnel. The famed Bear Mountain Bridge, completed in 1924, punctuates this especially picturesque portion of the Hudson valley. This suspension bridge carries Highway 6 and the Appalachian Trail across the river. Then at Garrison, the line passes another short tunnel, while

Above: The Hudson is often described as America's Rhine. Amtrak's Adirondack races southward along the Hudson at Bannermans Castle near Cold Spring, New York.

passengers can view the West Point military academy on the far side of the river. Further north, beyond Cold Spring, the line runs opposite Storm King Mountain, and it passes short parallel tunnels at Breakneck Ridge – a rock outcropping rising 1,260 feet (384 m) above the river. It was here that New York Central used to pose its famous limiteds for photography. 'Limiteds' refers to New York Central's finest passenger trains – such as the *Twentieth Century Limited*, previously mentioned, but also named trains such as its famed *Lake Shore Limited*, *Commdore Vanderbilt* and *Empire State Express*. These were stopped, posed and photographed by the railroad's company photographer Ed Novak at Breakneck Ridge and the images widely distributed. Today's passengers might recognize the location because of its fame from these historic images. Bannermans Castle sits on an island off the east bank of the river.

Beyond, to Albany, the scenery remains pleasant, but is less dramatic. North of the Poughkeepsie station, the line passes below the immense cantilever span that once carried the New Haven Railroad's Maybrook Line. Last used for freight in 1973, this bridge is now a popular footpath. Beyond Poughkeepsie the railway is in excellent condition, and allows for some very fast running. This is a great opportunity to find a seat in the diner and enjoy a classic meal on the final lap of the journey to Albany!

Below: A southward Empire Service train catches the summer evening sun along the Hudson at Castleton, New York. Today Amtrak's frequent passenger trains fulfil the role historically performed by New York Central's 'Great Steel Fleet'. Although swift, safe and comfortable, Amtrak's trains lack the glamour and elegance of Central's famous Limiteds.

OVER THE OLD 'BROAD WAY'

New York to Pittsburgh via the Juniata Valley
and the Horseshoe Curve

Brian Solomon

The Pennsylvania Railroad (PRR) was America's greatest transportation company in its heyday. It operated more than 10,000 miles (16,000 km) of railroad – connecting New York, Philadelphia and Washington, D.C. with Chicago, Pittsburgh, Cincinnati and St. Louis, and dozens of smaller cities across the northeast and midwest. The railroad handled such a volume of freight and passenger traffic that most of its 'Main Line' across Pennsylvania and New Jersey was expanded to four tracks and was known as its 'Broad Way' (no relation to New York City's famous avenue). PRR's Northeast electrification – energized at 11,000 volts alternating current – made it the most intensive electrified railway in North America (covering 671 route miles/1,080 route km, representing 2,252 track miles/3,624 track km). PRR was America's premier passenger railroad, in 1952 carrying more than 74 million passengers, and offering dozens of named trains across its network. Most famous was its flagship *Broadway Limited* that connected New York City and Philadelphia with Chicago via Pittsburgh and Crestline, Ohio, named ambiguously after both the route and its New York destination.

Today, Amtrak's *Pennsylvanian* traces the heart of the old PRR Main Line. You may join the train at Manhattan's Penn Station and travel under the Hudson River through PRR's famous tunnels, then down the Northeast Corridor across New Jersey – America's busiest passenger railway, shared with NJ Transit and Pennsylvania's SEPTA – to Philadelphia. Alternatively, begin your journey in Philadelphia, for many years the location of PRR's general offices. In 1933 PRR

Opposite: Just after sunrise on a June morning the view from Tunnel Hill in Gallitzin, Pennsylvania finds an uphill Norfolk Southern carload freight passing an intermodal container train that is drifting down 'The Slide'. The old PRR 'Broad Way' remains a heavily travelled freight corridor.

completed its magnificent two-level 30th Street Station west of Center City Philadelphia. Considered one of the last great American railway terminals, 30th Street blends classical design with art deco motifs. Its Corinthian colonnade makes for a grand gateway to one of America's most historic cities. In the immense main concourse a titanic bronze angel offers a haunting commemoration to PRR employees killed during the Second World War. Long-distance trains are boarded below the concourse. If you arrived from New York City, you'll notice that the *Pennsylvanian* changes direction at Philadelphia retracing its path a couple of miles back to Zoo Junction where it then heads west on the railroad's traditional Main Line.

As the train rolls west, you pass Rosemont, Paoli and Exton. Here one of PRR's freight cut-offs, which had allowed heavy freights to avoid the grades coming out of Philadelphia, joined the Main Line. At the village of Gap, the railroad navigates a deep cutting and takes a sharp bend, then traverses Pennsylvania Dutch country, where Amish and Mennonite farmers maintain their historic traditions. You might see their horse-drawn carriages as you zip along under wire. At Paradise, the Strasburg Rail Road connects with the Main Line – this short line is the oldest in the United States operating under its original charter. Today, the railway is largely a steam-hauled tourist line and you might see one of its historic steam locomotives at the junction or crossing the fields to the west.

There are station stops at Lancaster and Middletown – the location of another historic short line railway, the Middletown & Hummelstown – before reaching the state capital at Harrisburg. Electrification ends here; while Amtrak's *Keystone Corridor* trains use electric power to Harrisburg, the *Pennsylvanian* may switch its electric engine for a diesel at either 30th Street or Harrisburg depending on which better suits operations. Historically, electrification extended across the Susquehanna River to Enola for PRR's freight services but this was discontinued by Conrail in the early 1980s.

Right: Amtrak train 42, the Pennsylvanian, works upgrade at Lilly, Pennsylvania on its way from Pittsburgh to Philadelphia. In its heyday, the Pennsylvania Railroad scheduled more than 20 passenger trains each way daily. Today, Amtrak operates just one, yet the line remains busy with freight.

Continuing west from Harrisburg, the *Pennsylvanian* avoids the massive freight classification yards at Enola and runs northward to PRR's traditional crossing of the Susquehanna at Rockville. Originally, a wooden Howe-truss, the bridge was replaced twice and since 1902 has consisted of a 48-span stone arch viaduct, making it the world's largest continuous stone bridge over a river. The views up and down the Susquehanna are breathtaking. Important junctions with former PRR freight lines are located at both ends of the bridge.

West of Rockville, the *Pennsylvanian* shares the line with dozens of Norfolk Southern freights, as this remains one of the principal freight corridors in the eastern United States. Traditionally, PRR routed some freight east towards Philadelphia but in the 1970s Conrail diverted most through-freight to other routes east of Enola. As you roll west along the Susquehanna and Juniata River valleys you will pass and overtake many long trains heavily laden with shipping containers, traditional freight cars and coal hoppers.

The Juniata Valley is among the scenic highlights of the run. In the 1840s and 1850s, this line was surveyed and built by PRR's brilliant engineer, J. Edgar Thomson, later the railroad's third president. In places the line hugs the Juniata, in others it crosses fields and runs along mountain ridges. You pass many historic towns, making stops at Lewistown and Huntingdon, where you can see vintage PRR stations on the north side of the track (right side of the train travelling west). PRR's original alignment through Huntingdon was different from today's, so its old station is set back from the current platform. In the 1990s, the station was brightly repainted in its original Victorian-era colours.

Situated at the base of the Allegheny Divide (Eastern Continental Divide), Altoona was at the heart of the old PRR. Here the railroad had extensive yards and principal locomotive shops where it built many of its own locomotives,

Above: *This immense bronze sculpture of an angel at Philadelphia's 30th Street Station commemorates Pennsylvania Railroad employees who lost their lives in the Second World War.*

among them its famous K4s Pacifics that led the railroad's passenger trains in the classic era. In their heyday, its shops employed thousands of men and were the main employer in the region. Although much smaller than in the days of steam, the shops survive and today repair Norfolk Southern diesels. Another part of the complex, located across from Altoona's modest passenger station, houses the Altoona's Railroaders Museum, which has title to one of two surviving K4s Pacifics that it hopes to restore to service. (The small 's' indicates that the engine was 'superheated', and doesn't imply a plural.)

Beyond Altoona is the most spectacular part of the line. To ascend the divide, J. Edgar Thomson engineered the line into Burgoon Run on the famous alignment known worldwide as 'the Horseshoe Curve' because of its distinctive profile. To appreciate this wonder of 19th-century railroading, it is best to sit on the left side of the train heading west. PRR landscaped the centre of the Curve and it remains as a public attraction where visitors come to watch the continual procession of freight trains struggling up the mountain. The gradient requires most freights to take on 'helper' locomotives at Altoona to assist with the tonnage, so you'll see and hear engines roaring away at both ends of the train. Yet, to the passenger, it seems like a relatively gentle climb compared with highway crossings of the divide. Beyond Horseshoe Curve you can gaze to the left across the valley of Sugar Run where, on the far side, trucks labour up State Highway 22.

At Gallitzin the railroad ducks into tunnels at the Allegheny Divide. Beyond that, the line descends towards Johnstown, passing the villages of Cresson, Lilly, Cassandra, Portage and South Fork. The old steel centre of Johnstown is famous for its great flood of May 1889, when a dam near South Fork burst, sending forth a roaring wall of water that brought destruction to the Little Conemaugh Valley, sweeping whole trains off the tracks and drowning some 3,000 hapless souls. Today, Pittsburgh is the end of the run for the *Pennsylvanian*. Historically, PRR's passenger trains continued west. Now Amtrak's *Capitol Limited* provides connections to Chicago but this uses the old New York Central route west of Cleveland.

THE OLD RIO GRANDE NARROW GAUGE

Cumbres & Toltec and Durango & Silverton

Brian Solomon

At the end of the American Civil War, Union general Jackson Palmer migrated west to Colorado, where he began to put into action his plan of building a railway network connecting Denver with Santa Fe and Mexico City. Building a railway across the rugged terrain of the Colorado Rockies presented its fair share of challenges, so Palmer embraced narrow gauge to reduce construction and operation costs. The narrow width of the tracks allowed for tighter curves and required lesser earthworks to provide an adequate alignment.

Over the years the name of the railroad evolved and in the end, long after Palmer's time, it was called the Denver & Rio Grande Western, generally known as the 'Rio Grande'. In the 1870s and 1880s, as Rio Grande extended lines across the Rockies, its focus changed to embrace the Colorado mining boom. Rio Grande's San Juan extension reached Durango, Colorado, in 1881, by way of Cumbres Pass, and it was one of many Colorado lines to crest 10,000 feet (3,000 m).

By the 1890s, difficulties with interchanging cars for transcontinental connections encouraged Rio Grande to begin conversion of its main east-west routes to standard gauge, yet its network of lines tapping Colorado's mineral wealth continued as narrow gauge. A few of these routes survived, complete with steam power, into the late 1960s, making them among the last narrow-gauge common carrier routes in North America. After common carrier service ended, Colorado and New Mexico jointly preserved the route that connects Antonito, Colorado and Chama, New Mexico as the most scenic 64-mile (103-km) section.

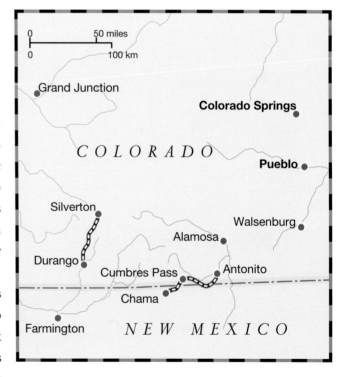

Opposite: At Chama, New Mexico, ash pans are cleaned on former Denver & Rio Grande Western 2-8-2 'Mikado' 489 in preparation for the day's work on the Cumbres & Toltec Scenic Railroad.

Today the Cumbres & Toltec Scenic (C&TS) Railroad offers seasonal excursions between Antonito and Chama using authentically restored former Rio Grande 2-8-2 'Mikado' steam locomotives. (Rio Grande's Silverton Branch, part of this former narrow-gauge network, was also preserved – see Durango & Silverton below.)

West from Antonito, the C&TS line meanders across high desert covered in sage brush on its ascent of the Rockies. A short distance out of town it crosses a wooden pile bridge known as 'Hangman's Trestle', harking back to the lawless days of the old West. To gain elevation, the line snakes left and then right, giving passengers the opportunity to look back on the tracks they have just travelled. The high desert plateau gives way to mountainous forest as the line reaches the rim of the wild and rocky Toltec Gorge. In places, the tracks cling precariously to cliff sides, in others the line cuts in away from the edge of the gorge, but the vistas remain captivating as the Toltec River roars hundreds of feet below the tracks.

In normal operations, trains from Antonito meet trains working east from Chama at the remote station at Osier on the east slope of Cumbres Pass. Trains continuing west then ascend the 10,000-foot (3,000-m) summit, working their way through the sinuous 'whiplash curve', where the line loops back on itself to gain elevation over the pass. At the summit, there is a turning 'wye', where helper engines can reverse after working the steep climb from Chama. From here, westward trains would begin their cautious descent down the line, past Windy Point and into New Mexico. Unfortunately, Cumbres & Toltec can only offer a truncated service at present because a disastrous fire in 2010 destroyed its Lobato trestle – the railroad's second tallest bridge – located just east of Chama. It is hoped that soon the bridge will be repaired, so that passengers can again enjoy the difficult eastward ascent of Cumbres Pass, which has long been one of the highlights of the run.

Opposite: Former Denver & Rio Grande Western class K27 2-8-2 463 – a type known as a 'Mudhen' – leads a double headed excursion at the summit of Cumbres Pass. The 'Mudhen' will cut off here, turn on the 'wye', and return to Chama, while the rest of the train will continue to Antonio.

Above: Cumbres & Toltec class K36 'Mikado' leads an excursion over Hangman's Trestle on the way to Antonito. The high desert at the east end of the run makes for relatively easy going compared with the rugged terrain over Cumbres Pass and along the Toltec Gorge.

Left: Cumbres & Toltec Scenic features a difficult steep ascent of Cumbres Pass, including the climb to Windy Point, where locomotives must be worked extra hard to haul trains upgrade.

Durango & Silverton

Rio Grande's 33-mile (53-km) Durango & Silverton(D&S) branch connected its namesake towns supporting a late 19th-century mining boom at the latter point. Located in a remote mountain valley, Silverton served as a hub for mining operations in the region with branch railways penetrating deeper into the mountains to tap silver mines.

Railroad traffic consisted of men and materials needed for silver mining, as well as mine outputs. Mine traffic tapered off in the 20th century but the branch survived. By the 1940s, Rio Grande's narrow-gauge network was in steep decline, with remaining lines subsisting on freight business. In 1951, it discontinued its famous *San Juan* – the last scheduled, named narrow-gauge passenger train. This left its tri-weekly Durango to Silverton mixed train as the only remaining narrow-gauge passenger service. Despite efforts to discontinue this run, the spectacular nature of the line continued to attract passengers. In a reversal of policy, Rio Grande decided to develop the line as a tourist attraction and ever since it has flourished, setting an important precedent for scenic railways elsewhere.

Above: Seasonally, Durango & Silverton operates multiple daily round trips between its Colorado namesake towns. On a late summer evening a D&S hugs the rim of the Animas Canyon on its return trip to Durango.

Although Durango & Silverton is no longer operated by the Rio Grande (the narrow gauge was sold decades ago, while standard-gauge sections of old Denver & Rio Grande Western became part of Southern Pacific in 1988, and then SP was absorbed by Union Pacific in 1996), the line is still operated independently with authentic Rio Grande steam locomotives similar to those that serve the C&TS (see above). The highlight of the run is the exceptionally deep and narrow Animas Canyon, where the line has been cut into a rocky shelf high above the river. This remote and very scenic cliff is isolated from highway transport and much of it can only be seen by railroad. In season, D&S operates several round trips from Durango, which serves as their base of operation. Enjoy the return trip down the Canyon of Lost Souls, where the syncopated clickety-clack of wheels over rail joints, steam exhaust and occasional haunting, howling whistle place you in a live performance of the American blues. It is best experienced on a rainy autumn evening which accentuates the sounds and the coal aroma from the locomotive.

CONWAY SCENIC'S CRAWFORD NOTCH

Into the White Mountains on the old Maine Central

Brian Solomon

New Hampshire's White Mountains provide the setting for one of New England's most spectacular railway journeys. The Conway Scenic Railroad operates the former Maine Central's Mountain Division over Crawford Notch – a line with almost mystical appeal. Built as the Portland and Ogdensburg in an effort to connect the Atlantic port with the St Lawrence Valley, the route originally stretched from Portland, Maine to the railway hub at St Johnsbury, Vermont. It reached 1,900 feet (579 m) above sea level at the top of Crawford Notch. After the line opened in 1874, the area was developed as a 19th-century resort community and benefited from considerable tourist traffic coming by rail to visit hotel spas. Boston & Maine and Maine Central offered joint services.

The station at Fabyan served the famed Mt Washington Hotel at Bretton Woods, while at Crawford Notch itself a beautiful Queen Anne-style station was built in 1891 to serve passengers visiting the scenically situated Crawford House Hotel. Although the hotel burned down in 1977, the classic station survives. Scheduled passenger services ended in the 1950s, though Maine Central continued to operate the line as a freight route until 1983 when it closed the line in favour of other routes. While not as awe-inspiring as the Rocky Mountain railways, the scenery on the line is as majestic as the famous Colorado narrow-gauge lines. As a mainline grade, it was unusually steep for a line in the eastern United States, with portions of the route exceeding 2 per cent.

Public interest in the line and its spectacular scenery led the Conway Scenic Railroad, based at North

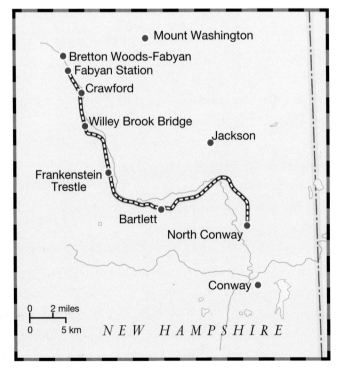

Conway, New Hampshire, to reopen the route in the 1990s. Since the 1970s Conway Scenic had offered historic excursions on portions of a former Boston & Maine branch. Today's seasonally operated excursion train resembles a classic 1950s streamliner and includes a Budd-built glass-topped Vista Dome (which calls for an extra fare). The train departs North Conway on the former B&M, and runs a short distance north to the junction with the Maine Central route, and then proceeds westward towards Crawford Notch.

Above: Conway Scenic's excursion train led by former Canadian National FP9 diesels pauses at Crawford Notch. This was a though freight route as late as 1983, but today survives as one of New England's most scenic tourist lines.

Climbing, the tracks cling to a shelf against sheer rock face while spanning gorges on towering trestles. Most famous are the Frankenstein and Willey Brook Trestles that offer some of the most dramatic mountain views. The most stunning vistas are available from the right side of the train. In places it seems as if the line rides on tree tops, with the landscape dropping off sharply below the wheels. Deep down in the valley Highway 312 – Crawford Notch Road – follows the line. While short excursions are operated from North Conway on former B&M routes, Notch trains are scheduled from June to October. Mid-autumn is the best time to ride; foliage turns from green to golden and ruby shades that contrast sharply with the grey granite cliffs, and the days range from crisp, bright sun to misty, mysterious, mountain-clinging fog punctuated by shafts of golden sunlight.

MAINE EASTERN'S ROCKLAND BRANCH

Downeast Delight

Brian Solomon

Among the most picturesque railways in New England is the former Maine Central Rockland Branch that runs for 57 miles (92 km) between Brunswick and its namesake coastal town. Proposed back in 1849, the difficult terrain and numerous crossings of coastal estuaries and rivers delayed the opening of the line until 1872. Historically the railroad served as a common carrier connecting Maine fishing villages with the rest of the nation. Freight on the line consisted of limestone from Rockland quarries, granite from Vinylhaven island, cement from the Dragon Cement works in Thomaston and general merchandise. Fish and lobsters were carried in baggage cars aboard passenger trains for rapid delivery to east coast markets. Passenger trains consisted of all-stops locals as well as seasonal through-trains from both Boston and New York.

Opposite above: A westward Maine Eastern excursion crosses the plate-girder deck bridge over the Mill River Estuary east of Thomaston, Maine. The scenic splendour of coastal Maine is among the finest in the eastern USA.

Opposite below: Seasonally, Maine Eastern operates two scheduled round trips daily over the historic former Maine Central Rockland Branch. At Rockland, passengers inspect a former New Haven Railroad FL9 used to operate excursions.

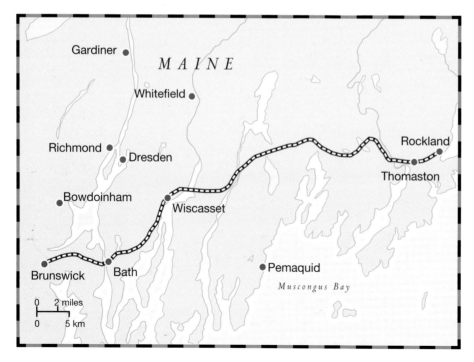

These accommodated holiday travellers and tourists who enjoyed vacationing at Maine's coastal resorts.

When trains didn't carry through-cars, passengers changed trains at Portland Union Station, where Maine Central met Boston & Maine. The winding nature of the branch and numerous bridges and frequent stations meant that most trains ran at a relatively leisurely pace. In 1949 the morning local departed Portland at 8.25 a.m. After travelling 84 miles (135 km), it arrived at Rockland at 11.12 a.m. In the early 1950s, steam gave way to diesels, and by the end of the decade all but freight services had been discontinued. In the 1980s the branch reached its nadir, and freight service had become alarmingly infrequent, with weeks passing between runs. Fortunately local efforts to preserve the line in the 1980s and 1990s were successful.

Today the railway is run by Maine Eastern, which provides freight service year-round and a seasonal scheduled passenger service using restored 1940s and 1950s era streamlined cars hauled by vintage locomotives, typically streamlined FL9s built for the New Haven Railroad. Weekend service begins on the weekend including Memorial Day (the last Monday in May), with a full weekday service operating in the summer consisting of two round trips between Rockland and Brunswick. In addition, stops are made at Wiscasset and Bath. Parlour car service is offered for an extra fee.

There are many scenic highlights along the line with the best views from the south side of the train (the left side when travelling west from Rockland). Railway enthusiasts will note the traditional roundhouse and turntable on the right-hand side of the tracks shortly after departing Rockland. Here locomotives are turned after most runs. A few miles later is the enormous Dragon Cement plant which generates most of the line's freight traffic. At Thomaston the train passes the old Maine Central station – one of the oldest structures on the line that originally was servants' quarters for the nearby General Henry Knox mansion. There are many interesting bridges along the route, and extensive views of coastal waterways. At Wiscasset the line crosses a series of fills along the Sheepscot River. The 19th-century village at Wiscasset is generally considered Maine's 'prettiest'. At Bath the line crosses the lower deck of the Carleton Bridge over the Kennebec River. This historic town and Bath Iron Works lie on the west side of this span. Prior to its construction in 1927, whole trains, complete with locomotives, were ferried across the Kennebec. Since the rehabilitation of the line in the early 2000s, the journey over the old Rockland Branch is smooth and pleasant. Round trips can be enjoyed from any of the four stations along the line.

Above: *Maine Eastern's excursion train uses equipment typical of 1950s streamliners that once connected many American cities. The sun catches the train at Rockland's stub end station – a facility rebuilt in recent years after many years of disuse.*

VIA RAIL'S CHALEUR

A Coastal Cruise without a Boat

George Pitarys

The Gaspé peninsula is a 200-mile (322-km) long finger of land stretching into the North Atlantic Ocean. Its north shore constitutes the south bank of the St Lawrence River, which is the world's largest estuary and outlet for North America's Great Lakes. The Gaspé peninsula joins the mainland at Matapédia, Quebec – situated at the confluence of the Restigouche and Matapédia rivers – while Chaleur Bay forms its south shore. Its namesake city of Gaspé lies at its northeastern tip and this point is the terminus for *The Chaleur* VIA Rail Canada train number 16.

The train's normal off-season consist is an F40PH diesel-electric locomotive, a baggage car, a coach, a Skyline dome car (where on-board meals are served) and two Château series sleeping cars. These cars were built for Canadian Pacific Railway (CPR) in 1954 by Philadelphia-based Budd Company using their trademark fluted stainless steel style. They were ordered when CPR revamped its passenger services and introduced a new flagship, streamlined, transcontinental train, *The Canadian*. *The Chaleur* actually begins in Montreal as a part of *The Ocean* – VIA's Montreal–Halifax train (see page 58); however, at peak travel times *The Chaleur* may operate independently of *The Ocean* and may double in size.

Three times a week, in the early morning hours of Monday, Thursday and Saturday these trains are separated at Matapédia, Quebec, and *The Chaleur* leaves for the Gaspé coast. Soon a magnificent mountain range comes into view to the north and west of the railway. This is the northern extreme of the Appalachian range that runs parallel to the coast at varying distances; sometimes a few miles away and at others coming right to the water's edge. Generally the railway line runs on the strip of land between the coast and the mountains, and where the mountains abut the shore, the ride and views are most spectacular.

Opposite: Bathed in early morning light, The Chaleur glides along by the blue waters of its namesake bay at Carleton, Quebec. Even though it's early April, snow still lingers.

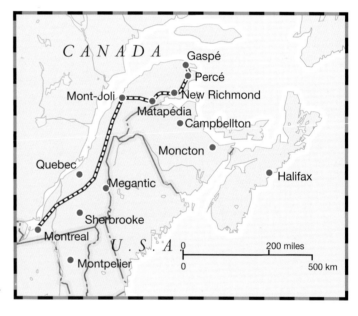

Opposite: The curved trestle at Prevel is about 125 feet (38 m) high and 700 feet (213 m) long. Although there are numerous trestles of a similar size along the entire Gaspé route, this is the only one with a curve. Crossing it is exhilarating.

From Matapédia to New Richmond there are a number of short stretches where the tracks hug the water line – notably from Matapédia to Pointe à la Croix and from Carleton to Maria – but in most places the line takes a more inland course through farmlands and spruce forest. In autumn, the higher slopes of the mountains are resplendent with hardwood foliage. Particularly colourful are the bright orange and red of the maple trees. From New Richmond onwards the shore running becomes more and more frequent and extended. At some places you are nearly at beach level and at others you will ride cliff sides a hundred or more feet above the water.

Above: An experienced photographer takes advantage of the splendid viewing platform provided by the dome car, as the The Chaleur passes sea ice a few miles west of Gaspé.

Quaint villages are encountered frequently along the way, and among them is Port Daniel where the track curves around a bay clustered with lobster boats and fishing trawlers. Beyond Port Daniel, the train passes through a 630-foot (192-m) long tunnel that cuts through a headland. Later it crosses a series of trestle bridges over estuaries and valleys. While some of these bridges are short and low to the ground, others are hundreds of feet long and more than 100 feet (30 m) tall.

Through the towns of Chandler, Pabos, Grand Rivière and Percé the ocean is very near at hand with spectacular vistas as the train cruises along tracks so close to the shore that looking down from the dome you will see only water! In particular, look for the famous Percé Rock as you approach Ste Thérèse. This island has a sheer rock formation containing one of the largest and most spectacular natural arches in the world, literally a 50-foot (15-m) high hole through the middle of the island.

Beyond Percé the railroad crosses the mountain range, then regains its place along the sea at Coin du Banc. In the final 25-mile (40-km) lap to Gaspé the line crosses two long causeways at Barachois and Douglastown. There's also a notable high curved trestle at Prevel.

The trip from Matapédia to Gaspé is just over 200 miles (322 km) and takes six hours and 50 minutes. Although the train runs at a sedate pace, you'll be in no hurry for this trip to end!

Opposite above: The westbound Chaleur is skimming along on top of the red cliffs at Caplan, Quebec. This scene and landscape are common along the many miles while the train traces the coastline.

Opposite below: At some points the train is far above the ocean, such as this view from the dome at Gascons illustrates. The viewer is looking northeast towards the open North Atlantic Ocean.

VIA RAIL'S OCEAN

Canadian History on an Overnight Train

George Pitarys

*T*he *Ocean* is a VIA-operated train that runs between Montreal, Quebec and the great port city of Halifax, Nova Scotia. But *The Ocean* is a lot older than VIA: in fact it was inaugurated in July 1904 and, at 109 years, is the longest-running continually named train in North America.

Three days a week – Wednesday, Friday and Sunday – *The Ocean* leaves Montreal, while on Tuesdays, Fridays and Sundays a train departs Halifax for the overnight journey. The train consists of Eurostar cars originally built for Chunnel service which VIA purchased a decade ago. There is the normal complement of coach, dining and sleeping cars. In the high summer season a Park car (a domed observation lounge car) is added. This has a dome at the forward part of the car, beneath that are three double bedrooms and a triple bedroom. Behind and beneath the dome is a large lounge area, which is rounded rather than square at the end of the car. The Park car always runs on the rear of the train. For all three trips, the train will also have *The Chaleur* (VIA's Gaspé train, see page 54) attached ahead of the Halifax section of the train.

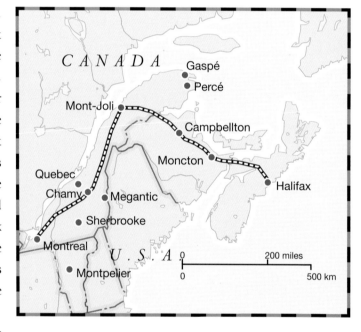

Using the eastbound No 14 as the example, the train departs Montreal at dinnertime and runs parallel to the St Lawrence River for some distance, arriving by late evening at Charny. Here, if you know where to look, you can see across the river to Quebec City and to the Plains of Abraham where General James Wolfe defeated Montcalm's French troops in 1759, so determining that Canada would be English rather than New France. The spot is just east of the rather large freight yards through which the train passes right after the (eastward) station stop at Charny. (If travelling west, look out on the north side of the train 15–20 minutes before the Charny station arrival time.) You might also see the lights of the famous Château Frontenac where in 1943 Franklin

Opposite: The Ocean *whips across the salt marshes at the tip of the Bay of Fundy near the New Brunswick and Nova Scotia border. It is all 'Renaissance' equipment except a Park car on the rear which is added to the summer consist.*

D. Roosevelt and Winston Churchill met and together planned the invasion of Nazi Germany.

As the night unfurls, the train passes Rimouski where just offshore the liner RMS *Empress of Ireland* was involved in a collision and sank in May 1914 with the loss of over 1,000 lives, a death toll that rivalled those of the *Titanic* and *Lusitania*.

As morning approaches, on those scheduled days, *The Chaleur* will split off at Matapédia, Quebec, and you can observe daybreak as you cruise down the beautiful southern edge of Chaleur Bay. By lunch the city of Moncton has come and gone as the train nears the border with Nova Scotia. Here, the route skirts the northern tip of the Bay of Fundy, home of the largest tides in the world, where the difference in water level between low and high tide can vary by as much as 48 feet (14.6 m)!

Below: 685 miles (1,102 km) and 18 hours into its journey the eastbound Ocean is approaching Sackville in the heavily wooded province of New Brunswick. The miles of spruce forest that are seen play an important role in the economy of much of Eastern Canada.

Opposite: More than 20 of the Budd-built stainless steel cars comprise The Ocean on this day as it speeds across the flats near Upper Dorchester, New Brunswick.

Opposite: The early morning sun glints off an all-stainless-steel eastbound Ocean which is passing the beach at Nash Creek, New Brunswick on the southern shore of Chaleur Bay.

By late afternoon Bedford Basin, Halifax's inner harbour, comes into view and suddenly, 22 hours after departure, the great port is there. Halifax is where survivors and victims of the *Titanic* sinking were brought and many are buried here. There is a great museum called 'The Maritime Museum of the Atlantic' and a historic fort known as the Citadel which was the British garrison until 1906 and from which a ceremonial cannon is still fired daily at noon. This is Halifax, the port from which so many Second World War North Atlantic convoys set sail, and now a great place to visit and meet friendly Nova Scotians proud of the city and its heritage.

VIA RAIL'S CANADIAN

VIA's Transcontinental Flagship

George Pitarys

In April 1955 in a last-ditch effort to recapture a rapidly dwindling passenger clientele, both major Canadian railways, the Canadian Pacific (CP) and the Canadian National (CN), inaugurated new transcontinental services. The CN called its new train *The Super Continental*, while the CP named theirs *The Canadian*. Both companies made substantial investments in new equipment. The CP bought 173 fluted stainless steel cars from the Budd company of Philadelphia, Pennsylvania that included baggage cars, coach, dining and sleeper cars, Skyline (glass-domed) cars and domed observation lounge sleeping cars.

Passenger numbers, however, continued to decline and in the late 1970s a crown corporation named VIA was formed which took over the floundering passenger services of CP and CN. Equipment was intermingled and some new locomotives were purchased. Services were consolidated as well, although both transcontinental routes remained intact, until 14 January 1990 that is, when the last Canadian Pacific 'Canadian' departed Montreal for Vancouver. For reasons that are still somewhat obscure, VIA chose the CN route over the CP route but kept the name *The Canadian* for the transcontinental service. Fortunately they also

Opposite: A wooden grain elevator stands watch over the eastbound Canadian *as it makes its station stop at the small prairie community of Rivers, Manitoba. Once numbering in the thousands, many of these classic buildings have been razed or abandoned. As always a Park observation car is bringing up the rear of* The Canadian.

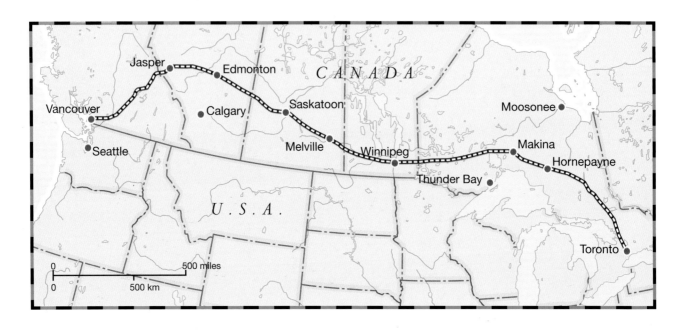

retained and refurbished the vintage Budd equipment that CP had purchased for the original train. The train's size varies with the season from a minimum of about nine cars in the winter to as many as 28 cars in the summer.

Long considered to be one of the premier rail journeys in North America, the trip across Canada is far more than a passage through the beautiful Canadian Rocky Mountains – the aspect most frequently associated with the trip – it is, at 2,775 miles (4,466 km) and spanning five days, the longest single train journey in North America. It entails a crossing of that continent with all its rich diversity.

Using the westbound trip as a template, on day one, the journey begins in Toronto, Ontario, Canada's largest metropolitan area with over 5.1 million inhabitants. Westbound VIA train number one, *The Canadian*, departs late on Tuesday, Thursday and Saturday evenings from May 1 to Oct 31, and Tuesdays and Saturdays only from Nov 1 to April 30. (The eastbound counterpart number two departs Vancouver on Tuesday, Friday and Sunday evenings from May 1 to Oct 27, and Tuesdays and Fridays only from Oct 28 to April 30).) As the lights of the city disappear, first-class travellers share a champagne toast and most soon retire to their sleeping quarters.

By morning of day two, passengers awaken in the boreal forests of the Canadian shield. This entire day, evening and night will be consumed in crossing the deep woods and pristine lakes of northern Ontario. Bear, moose, deer and other forest creatures are often seen from the dome car, of which two or more are spaced throughout the train.

Early on day three, the train crosses into the province of Manitoba and at 8 a.m. arrives in Winnipeg. Here, the train will remain for four hours while it is re-provisioned and serviced mechanically, as well as having the dome windows washed. During this time passengers may detrain if they choose to. Once underway again, the train is upon the vast prairie. For all of this day and part of the next the train will traverse nearly 1,000 miles (1,600 km) of rolling wheat fields, dotted with small towns and dozens of prairie grain elevators. It is a remarkable story of agricultural success, highlighted by the train's journey

Above: Once part of Canadian Pacific's chain of fine hotels, the Royal York is across the street from Toronto's Union Station, and is seen behind the Park car, which is on the rear of westbound train No 1, The Canadian. Soon that flagship train will start its thrice weekly, four-day journey across the continent.

which enables you to appreciate the enormity of this 'garden' in the provinces of Manitoba, Saskatchewan and Alberta.

By late in the morning of day four, the Rocky Mountains have come into view. Depending on the time of year, the peaks may be shrouded in snow, or in many cases covered by glaciers. The railway follows the rivers in the valleys and winds its way through the mountains. The train makes a stop at Jasper where access can be had to several of the national parks, or a car rented for a trip down the spectacular Icefields Parkway. As the train makes it way west from Jasper, it soon crosses into the province of British Columbia and passes within sight of Mt Robson, the highest peak in the Canadian Rockies at 12,972 feet (3,954 m). This is a very special passage of one of the world's great mountain ranges.

During much of the evening of the fourth day the train follows the course of the Fraser River as it races towards the Pacific at Vancouver and by mid morning of day five passengers too arrive in that large city on the largest ocean.

VIA recently extended the duration of the trip. Now lasting 84 hours, the journey across Canada on *The Canadian*, with its excellent dining and relaxing, scenery-filled days in the dome, is far more than simply the crossing of 2,775 miles (4,466 km): it's a true example of a journey being far more important than the destination.

Above: Named after an heroic First World War English nurse, 11,033-foot (3,363-m) Mt Edith Cavell looms on the horizon, while the eastbound Canadian is making its station stop at Jasper, Alberta. Jasper is the gateway to several of Canada's splendid national parks, as well as the connection for VIA's service to Prince Rupert, British Columbia named 'The Skeena'.

ROCKY MOUNTAINEER

Mountain Climbing in Comfort and Style

George Pitarys

On 7 November 1885 the last spike was driven in Canadian Pacific's quest to become transcontinental. The event occurred at Craigellachie, British Columbia, a place named after the ancestral Scottish home of the CP's first president, Sir George Stephen. The completion of the building of the Canadian Pacific included some amazing engineering feats during the surmounting of the Rocky and Selkirk mountain ranges.

Seventy years later, CP initiated a new transcontinental passenger service, which it named *The Canadian*. This service took advantage of some of the engineering triumphs in its passage of the southern Canadian Rockies. Among these were the spiral tunnels: two separate tunnels a few miles apart in which the railway track turns three-quarters of a complete circle within a mountain in order to gain or lose elevation. Long freight trains will cross over the top of themselves in the process of negotiating these tunnels. Also there was the Connaught Tunnel which, upon completion late in 1916, was – at 5.02 miles (8 km) in length – the longest railway tunnel in the Americas. This achievement was overtaken in the late 1980s by the 9.1-mile (14.6-km) long Mount MacDonald Tunnel (also on this route), presently the longest in the Americas.

Canadian Pacific, as the self-proclaimed 'world's greatest transportation system', owned numerous hotels across the country in addition to its fleet of ocean passenger liners and airlines. These included two world-renowned resorts in the Rockies that were serviced by its famous passenger train. The Banff Springs Hotel and the Chateau Lake Louise are still amongst the finest hotels in the country and the views from both, but particularly the Chateau Lake Louise, are magnificent.

Yet, despite all this infrastructure and historical significance, on 15 January 1990, compelled by governmental budgetary reductions, VIA was forced to

Opposite: Not long after leaving its eastern terminus at Calgary, Alberta, the westbound Rocky Mountaineer has begun its penetration of the 'Front Range' of the Rocky Mountains at Exshaw. The train, using the original Canadian Pacific route, will follow the Bow River valley through such fabled locations as Banff and Lake Louise.

implement its decision to abolish *The Canadian* on its traditional Canadian Pacific route. Apparently one the most spectacular railway journeys through the Canadian Rocky Mountains had been lost. Or so it seemed.

Prior to *The Canadian*'s discontinuance VIA had run a seasonal tourist train on the CP route called 'The Canadian Rockies by Daylight', later renaming it the *Rocky Mountaineer*. This concept, and name, was sold by VIA to a private corporation in April 1990, a few months after *The Canadian* had become history. So began one of the most successful tourist train operations in North America.

Today, with over 20 years of operation and more than a million passengers, Great Canadian Railtour Company operates the *Rocky Mountaineer* as well as four other trains that run to different destinations. There are approximately 45 departures per season (April until October) from Vancouver. The train's trip is a four-day journey, during which it runs from Vancouver, British Columbia to

Above: Four diesel-electrics lead a Rocky Mountaineer *tour train across Canadian Pacific's Nahatlatch River Bridge near Boston Bar, British Columbia. This scenic stretch of mainline is primarily used by CP's transcontinental freight trains; passengers can enjoy the line from the comfort of Rocky Mountaineer's high-end cruise trains which feature dome cars to view the scenery.*

Above right: In 1990, VIA Rail, Canada's national passenger rail operator, discontinued transcontinental services over the supremely scenic Canadian Pacific route in western Canada. Although an unfortunate loss of regular passenger service, this opened up opportunities for luxury cruise train service, now provided by Rocky Mountaineer. Their specially appointed train is seen in the narrow defile of the Fraser River Canyon, known as Hell's Gate, British Columbia.

Kamloops, BC where it overnights. All runs are made in daylight so that no scenery is missed. There are towering mountain peaks which most of the year will still have snow and/or glaciers atop them. The tracks also follow two rivers through deep valleys: the Bow that is a gently flowing river known for its good fishing and the Kicking Horse with a more turbulent flow.

On day two, the train splits at Kamloops and one section runs to Jasper, Alberta, while the other takes the CP's route to Calgary, Alberta. The trains layover at Jasper and Calgary on the second night, and, for passengers making the round trip, on day three return to Kamloops and once again tie up overnight. On the morning of day four, the trains recombine for the final leg of the trip back into Vancouver. This voyage between Kamloops and Calgary takes in all of the aforementioned engineering triumphs such as the Spiral tunnels, the MacDonald Tunnel and majestic bridges such as the Stony Creek arch. Once in danger of being seen only by freight-train crews, a journey on the *Rocky Mountaineer* now sets them all before the eyes of the general traveller.

The train may be ridden in either or both directions, and there is more than one level of service available. Depending on the level chosen, gourmet meals may be included in the package, as well as the overnight accommodation. This train travels what may very well be the most scenic railway route on the continent. A passage on the *Rocky Mountaineer*, successor to the legendary 'Canadian', is not cheap, but by the same token it is the trip of a lifetime and is, most surely, truly unforgettable.

WHITE PASS & YUKON

Scenic Railway of the World

Scott Snell

Gold Rush fever struck Alaska in 1897. The Klondike Gold Rush ushered in a wild time in a wild country. The sleepy town of Skaguay, changed to Skagway in 1899, was the main Alaskan port where eager prospectors seeking fame and fortune would disembark. Their main routes into the Klondike were the Chilkoot Pass and White Pass. Both were slow and treacherous, but that did not deter the eager fortune seekers. A better way to transport men and supplies northward was needed and the first tracks of the 110-mile (177-km) White Pass & Yukon Railway were laid in May 1898.

Led by Michael J. Heney, an Irish immigrant and labour contractor, rails of the WP&YR were soon crossing White Pass, elevation 2,865 feet (873 m). By the time the 3-foot (914-mm) gauge White Pass & Yukon reached its terminus of Whitehorse, Yukon, Canada in August 1900, the Gold Rush had all but ended. The WP&YR therefore focused on the transportation of other minerals including copper, silver and lead. Passengers were carried along the rails and also by a pair of steam-powered river boats. The White Pass did not play a major part in rail traffic during the First World War, and it managed to keep operating, on a limited basis, during the Great Depression. The Second World War, however, saw the railway assume a more important role. Alaska was recognized as strategically important due to its proximity to Japan. The US Army assumed operations of the railroad and the line was used to transport the bulk of the materials used in the construction of the Alaska Highway.

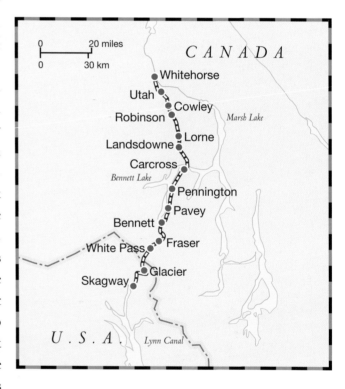

Returned to private ownership after the war, the White Pass began to replace its fleet of steam locomotives with diesels from General Electric, the American Locomotive Company and Montreal Locomotive Works during the mid to late 1950s. While most narrow-gauge systems in the United States were still operating

Opposite: White Pass & Yukon GE 90-class Shovel Nose diesels skirt the shores of Shallow Lake at Ptarmigan Point. Leading the train is locomotive No 98, the first of two 90-class units to be repowered with a new environmentally friendly engine.

with steam or abandoning operations all together, the White Pass modernized.

The 1960s brought major changes to the White Pass with an increase in passengers arriving in Skagway on cruise ships, then a major freight customer came online in 1969 with the opening of the Faro lead-zinc mine. The railroad was upgraded to handle the new traffic. However, the White Pass appeared to be heading for the end of the line when the Faro mine closed in 1982. With no freight remaining and only the passenger trains running, the railroad ceased operations in October 1982.

Negotiations between cruise operators and the railway resulted in a return of train services to the WP&YR in 1988. Trains initially operated only to the Summit due to labour and customs issues with Canada. Once these issues were resolved, trains operated all the way to Fraser, Yukon. Service continued on to Bennett in 1992 and trains once again reached Carcross in 2007.

Adjacent to the White Pass depot in Fraser is a beautifully restored enclosed wooden water tank. White Pass steam locomotives are still serviced from this historic structure.

In 1994 the White Pass & Yukon Railway was designated an International Historic Civil Engineering Landmark. The ride from Skagway to Fraser certainly proves the White Pass worthy of this honorary distinction. Spectacular views

Above: Dwarfed by the Coast Mountain Range, White Pass & Yukon Baldwin 2-8-2 Mikado-type No 73 steams south between Fraser, Yukon and Meadows, Yukon with a train from Bennett, Yukon bound for Skagway, Alaska. In the background is Bernard Lake.

greet the rider around every turn, some reaching as tight as 16 degrees. It is tough to figure out if one side of the train is preferable to the other. Historic narration is provided in each car, but a quiet car is also offered with no narrative. Passengers are allowed to ride the open vestibules between cars. This is a great way to take photographs along your journey and to listen to the locomotives working up the 3.9 per cent grade to the summit. The line climbs 2,865 feet (873 m) in the first 20 miles (32 km) out of Skagway.

It passes through two tunnels and over numerous small bridges and trestles. Rounding a curve near milepost 18, a massive steel bridge comes into view spanning Dead Horse Gulch and it appears as though the train is going to cross it, but the 840-feet (256-m) bridge hasn't seen a train since 1969! At the time of its construction in 1901, it was the largest steel cantilever bridge in the world. Trains now pass through a new tunnel to bypass the old bridge. Bridal Veil Falls at milepost 11.5 is another scenic highlight. Trains slow or make a brief stop here to view the 6,000-feet (1,830-m) cascading falls. Not far out of Skagway, trains also make a stop at the Denver Glacier Trail. Passengers can disembark and take the hike to the glacier and board a later train for the return to Skagway. A White Pass caboose is located here and is available to rent.

Above: Proudly advertising 'Gateway To The Yukon', a drumhead adorns the rear of a White Pass & Yukon Route passenger train awaiting departure from the railway's Skagway, Alaska depot.

White Pass & Yukon trains are hauled by both steam and diesel locomotives. Currently two steam locomotives are operable, No 69, a 2-8-0 built by Baldwin in 1908 and No 73, a 2-8-2 from Baldwin built in 1947. There are three different diesel models currently in use on the White Pass. The bulk of the fleet consists of the unique General Electric Class 90 Shovel Noses. Several of these units have been re-powered in recent years with a more environmentally friendly engine. The White Pass is committed to re-powering the 11-unit fleet. A fleet of eight ALCO-MLW DL-535E and a single DL-535E (W) round out the complement. The passenger car fleet of nearly 70 cars is a mix of restored wooden cars, the oldest being from 1889, and wood and steel replicas. The cars are all named after lakes and rivers in Alaska, the Yukon and British Columbia. All of the equipment is meticulously maintained at the railway's modern shop facilities at the north end of Skagway.

The busiest of all North American tourist railroads, the White Pass & Yukon set a record in July 2008, hauling 7,009 passengers in one day. Passengers are certainly big business for the White Pass, but the railway is looking to the future and the possibility of hauling freight once again. The White Pass is a unique link to the past, mixing the best of today and yesterday. Environmentally friendly diesels mixing it up with steam-powered trains on a torturous mountain railroad – today's traveller to Skagway won't be disappointed in their ride aboard the 'Scenic Railway of the World'.

MEXICO'S COPPER CANYON

A ride on North America's newest Transcontinental Railroad

Brian Solomon

Among the world's most famous railway journeys is the day-long passage through Mexico's Barranca del Cobre (Copper Canyon). Known for its stunning scenery and indigenous culture, this line attracts thousands of foreign visitors annually and is considered by many to be among the top world railway trips. The 406-mile (653-km) run from Los Mochis, Sinaloa to Chihuahua was the most difficult section of the route that was built from the US border to the Pacific port of Topolobampo. Conceived as a strategic transcontinental link in the 19th century, this railroad was more than six decades in the making, and was not completed until 1961. In 2011, the line celebrated its 50th anniversary.

During the mid-1990s, large portions of the Mexican railway network were privatized, and today the old Chihuahua–Pacifico route is operated by Ferrocarrill Mexicano – known as 'FerroMex'. However, Mexican passenger services had been in decline for decades, and by the 1990s accounted for less than 1 per cent of all intercity travel. Since then, federal subsidies for most intercity services were withdrawn, leaving only a handful of lines with regular services, including the ever-popular Copper Canyon route. Two services are operated under the name *El Chepe* (the name derives from its reporting mark CHP standing for Chihuahua–Pacifico); a first-class service runs daily, and a cheaper, slower, more economical train works three days a week to augment the first-class train.

El Chepe first-class trains are the preferred choice for most foreign travellers; these leave end terminals at 6 a.m. Many visitors prefer to ride from west to east, some join the train at El Fuerte allowing for a more civilized departure time than from Los Mochis. The journey begins in the tropical coastal valleys amid pastures

Opposite: The daily El Chepe *crosses the Río Fuerte on this multi-span deck truss bridge, one of 37 bridges on the spectacularly scenic run through Mexico's Barranca del Cobre.*

full of lush vistas of agricultural lands. The line climbs gently at first as it gradually ascends Mexico's mighty Sierra Madre range. Junctions at Sufragio and near San Blas connect the transcon-route with the north-south line between Nogales and Guadalajara. Mexican railways are primarily concerned with freight, and even on the scenic Copper Canyon line, it is normal to pass several freights. Since the route is largely single track with passing sidings from time to time, encounters with freights may result in minor delays. Unusual rock formations around El Fuerte are a prelude to the rugged territory ahead. East of the town the line crosses Río Fuerte on a spectacular multi-span deck truss 1,637 feet (499 m) long, the longest of 37 bridges on the line. Beyond Agua Caliente the line sinks into the inky gloom of El Descanso Tunnel – 6,033 feet (1,839 m) long, the biggest of the 86 tunnels that punctuate the journey.

Above: The old Chihuahua–Pacifico route is operated by Ferrocarrill Mexicano, premier passenger services are provided by the daily El Chepe *trains over the route through the* Barranca del Cobre, Copper Canyon.

The entire Barranca del Cobre system is four times larger than the Grand Canyon of the Colorado in Arizona, and is both longer and in parts deeper than the more famous American landmark. Scenically sublime, the Copper Canyon is known for its towering peaks and sinuous gorges. Yet the canyon is more wooded than the Grand Canyon, and populated by stands of conifers that cling to its steep walls and seem to blend into the deep shadows of its lower reaches. Among the highlights of the journey towards the summit are the loops at Témoris where the line follows an abnormally sinuous course to gain elevation. The region is famous for the Tarahumara, a native Mexican people noted for their agility as runners, unusual language and colourful dress, some of whom reside in cave dwellings in the canyons along the line.

Near the middle of the journey are choice stopover points for visitors wanting to extend their visit in the Copper Canyon. Divisadero is the highest station, and the village overlooks the rim of the canyon. Typically *El Chepe* trains meet here, and pause to allow visitors to wander around and stretch their legs mid-journey. Beyond, to the east, is the line's summit which crests just over 8,200 feet (2,499 m) above sea level, and represents the divide between the Copper and Ulrique Canyons. On the east slope is the village of Creel, which is a good place to enjoying the views and local culture, and even to stay overnight. As the line continues in a northeasterly direction, it winds and twists through stunning scenery.

Above: A train led by second-hand General Motors Electro-Motive Division locomotives departs the station at Creel heading for Mazatlan. Mexican railways have largely purchased both new and used railway equipment from American suppliers.

La Junta is both a station and the junction with a freight-only branch line. The next stop is Cuauhtémoc, a location famous for its Mennonite settlers, who speak German rather than Spanish. By the time the train finally arrives at Chihuahua, 15 hours or more from Los Mochis, most travellers are weary but enlightened. A trip through Copper Canyon tends to inspire a return journey because passengers are keen to experience its lofty crags and deep sinuous gorges one more time.

RAILS ALONG THE RHINE

A German Interlude

Brian Solomon

Railways sometimes seem to display an inverse relationship between beautiful scenery and traffic levels; in other words, highly scenic lines tend to have light traffic, while intensely used lines often pass through uninteresting scenery. There are a number of notable exceptions, however, among them the great German railways that operate along the Mittelrhein (Middle Rhine), where traffic levels and scenery are both exceptional.

Historically, the Rhine is one of the most significant rivers in Europe. Its headwaters begin high in the Swiss Alps and flow in a meandering path through Germany and the Netherlands to the North Sea near the port of Rotterdam. Over the centuries it has served both as a corridor and a barrier, a means of trade and a political boundary. At the time of Julius Caesar, the Rhine was viewed as marking the frontier between Rome and Celtic and Germanic lands to the north. Napoleon briefly established it as an eastern frontier; today portions of the river represent the border between Switzerland and its neighbours, and a portion marks the border between Germany and France. Yet despite many changes in European politics, today the Mittelrhein section resides entirely within Germany.

Having long served as a principal European trade route – much of the Rhine is still a major navigable waterway – it was only logical that main railways would follow its course. The route from Basle, Switzerland to Köln (Cologne) is among the most important intercity lines in north-central Europe. This not only sees a continual parade of local and intercity passenger trains, but is an increasingly busy freight corridor. Changes brought about by the European Union have opened up continental railways, and the important nature of Rhineland routes have made them attractive to a number of

freight operators. Where Deutsche Bahn (German Railways) was once the sole operator, now tracks are shared with a variety of companies, including freights run by SBB (Swiss Federal Railways).

There are many ways to approach a Rhine railway journey, depending on the time available, your personal level of interest and the direction of travel. This route is not a single railway line, but rather features several roughly parallel lines reaching various destinations. Since these lines are part of trans-European corridors, it is easy enough to incorporate a Rhineland journey as part of a bigger trip. The scenic splendour of the route is complemented by the region's rich history; the river valley is dotted with ancient fortifications and medieval castles while numerous historical towns and cities lie along the route. The casual traveller could easily spend a couple of weeks on the train wandering from town to town and never tiring of sights along the way. Likewise, a more hurried visitor can enjoy the highlights from the windows of an EC express train, making the run from Cologne to Stuttgart in just 3 hours 30 minutes.

Since the opening of the new 110-mile (177-km) Cologne–Frankfurt high-speed line in 2002, fast and frequent ICE (Intercity Express Services) race at regular intervals along this line instead of using the much slower Rhine valley lines. Some ICE trains continue to Basle and beyond on conventional lines. The

Above: This panoramic view from a terraced vineyard overlooking the broad expanse of the Mittlerhein east of Mainz finds a DB local passenger train accelerating away from its station stop at Rüdesheim am Rhein. Like European railways, DB has been phasing out traditional locomotive-hauled trains, but as of 2011 many survive on Rhine routes.

Above: *The scenic Rhine valley is a heavily travelled transport corridor; in addition to busy railway lines on both banks, the river sees a continual parade of passenger and cargo ships. A Railion freight rolls southwards near Braubach, Germany.*

wise traveller will opt to take the more scenic older route, as the new line sacrifices charm for expedience. Among the most convenient places to begin a journey down the Rhine is at Frankfurt airport, directly connected by two railway stations which makes transfers from plane to train unusually easy. Train times are displayed in the airport terminals, and railway tickets can be purchased to destinations across Europe. A more traditional starting point is the Frankfurt Hauptbahnhof (Main Station), one of Germany's classic terminals. Designed by Georg P.H. Eggert and completed in 1879, this stub-end station features a cavernous triple-span iron shed 610 feet (186 m) long, originally conceived to cover 18 tracks. If this station arrangement seems familiar, that's because its successful pattern was later emulated by many other stations across Europe and America.

Heading northwards along the Rhine from Frankfurt, travellers have a choice of using the left-bank route or the right. To enjoy a complete experience, plan a round trip out on one line and back on the other. Historically, express trains used the faster left-bank line, leaving the right bank for freights and all-stops locals. Today, freights and locals frequent both lines, although express trains are less frequent than they once were. The continual parade of trains makes for a great train-watching experience as you proceed down the river. Starting out in the morning from Frankfurt, consider going north on the right bank, and returning via the left, which suits the prevailing light conditions for most of the journey.

The Mittelrhein's scenic highlights are found in the sinuous gorge north of Mainz between Bingen and Koblenz. This is a recently designated UNESCO World Heritage Site and features the nicest scenery and most intriguing historic architectural delights. Near Kaub (on the right bank) is the famed Pfalzgrafenstein, a colourful castle situated on an island in the middle of the river. It was built in the 14th century by King of Germany and Holy Roman Emperor Ludwig IV to extort tolls from river ships. Today this is a very popular tourist attraction. Ferries from Kaub bring visitors to the island. Only a few miles up the river on the left bank is the historic walled town of Oberwesel, where the railway runs adjacent to ancient medieval towers. The walls are open to public, and few ancient venues offer better views of passing trains. Overlooking the town is the Schönburg Castle. One the characteristics of the Mittelrhein is the lack of bridges; in their place are a number of small ferries that shuttle cars and foot passengers back and forth across the river. One of these runs between St Goarshausen (on the left bank) and St Goar – a picturesque town settled in the 6th century, located near the 13th-century Burg Rheinfels (a picturesque ruined castle best viewed from the left bank).

At Boppard (on the left bank), the river makes a sharp S-bend, famous for its picturesque setting and difficult navigation. Here the left-bank railway ducks inland, as hotels and restaurant line the town's mile long 'Rheinallee' river-front promenade. Historically visitors used to arrive by river; by contrast, today many drive. Several nice hotels near the railway station make this an ideal place to stop for the night. Important since Roman times, historic baths dating to the period of the Roman occupation have been located beneath the main Marktplatz. Among the interesting ruins are a medieval castle tower adjacent to the railway.

Koblenz (corrupted from the Latin word meaning 'confluence') is where the Mosel (Moselle) River meets the Rhine. Railway bridges north and south of the city allow trains serving the right bank to access the Hauptbahnhof, and make this a desirable place to switch from one side of the river to the other. It is also the junction with the equally picturesque Mosel valley route to Trier and Luxembourg (see page 84). On the right bank, opposite the city, stands the

impressive Ehrenbreitstein citadel fortress. The views are a worth a side trip. The remainder of the journey towards Cologne is pleasant, with plenty of tranquil views of the river, but a little anticlimactic in comparison with the section just travelled. Bonn, Beethoven's birthplace and capital of the German Federal Republic through the Cold War years, makes for another interesting stop-over. Not far from Bonn on the right bank is Königswinter, location of the volcanic crag called Drachenfels (Dragon Rock) and the aptly named Drachenfelsbahn rack railway that takes visitors to the top.

The Cologne Hauptbahnhof is an impressive place at which to begin or conclude one's journey. This distinctive station was designed by J.E. Jacobstahl and represents an unusual European design, where the tracks are elevated above the street and the station is situated below the shed. Both station and Cologne's monumental cathedral that looms above were badly damaged during the Second World War, when 262 air raids rained bombs upon on the historic city. Happily both buildings have been repaired since that time.

The Mittelrhein's parallel left- and right-bank main lines connecting picturesque villages and towns combined with splendid scenic panoramas and classic architecture make for one of the most rewarding railway journeys in central Europe.

Above: A southward Trans-Regio electric local train makes a station stop at Boppard-Hirzenach on the Rhine's left bank. The village of Hirzenach is located at a bend in the Rhine a few miles south of the town of Boppard.

Opposite: Oberwesel, on the Rhine's west bank, exemplifies the historical character of the route. Here, the railway passes the old city walls, neatly squeezing between a pair of medieval towers.

MOSEL VALLEY

Through German Wine Country

Brian Solomon

From its headwaters high in the Vosges mountains in France, the River Mosel (in French Moselle) flows through one the most beautiful valleys in Europe, then meets the Rhine at the German city of Koblenz. A journey up the Mosel valley can make for a pleasant side trip when travelling along the Rhine, but it also deserves more extensive exploration if time allows. Like the Rhine, the Mosel is navigable and regularly scheduled river cruises can augment a railway journey. Locks along the river both facilitate commercial shipping while protecting the valley from periodic flooding. Similar in character to the Rhine, the lower Mosel valley is narrower, steeper and famously dotted with some of Germany's most romantic castles. Through-locomotive-hauled express InterCity trains that carry buffet cars operate on this route between Koblenz and Luxembourg on two-hour intervals throughout the day; while Regional Express trains run more frequently connecting Koblenz with Trier, and then head southward along the Saar Valley to Saarbrücken.

Not far from the Koblenz Hauptbahnhof (Main Station), the railway crosses the Mosel and closely follows the left bank for the next 31 miles (50 km). This is Germany's most famous wine-producing region, and terraced vineyards have been situated to take advantage of available south-facing slopes, some of them quite steep. Picturesque churches and castles dot the valley; about 10 miles (16 km) from Koblenz, the line skirts the walls of a small castle at Kobern-Gondorf, but the most famous of the castles along the route is Burg Eltz. This is perched on a hill above the river in the lush Eltzbachtal, not far from the station at Moselkern. Considered one of Germany's best and best-preserved medieval castles, this is a popular tourist attraction and the choice destination for many visitors. Those arriving by train face a 35-minute uphill walk. Despite this climb, visitors are rarely disappointed by either this 12th-century structure or the view from the top of it.

Also popular with visitors is the village of Cochem, where ample accommodation and restaurants cater to weary travellers and those wishing to experience more than a passing glance of the valley. Here the railway plunges into the 2.6-mile (4.2-km) Kaiser-Wilhelm Tunnel. The original bore dates to the 1870s, when it was the longest tunnel in Germany. A second bore is presently underway parallel to the first. The tunnel avoids a sinuous portion of the river and the line emerges near Ediger-Eller, where it crosses the river on a heavy deck bridge then plunges back underground via the short Petersberg Tunnel. Between the stations at Neef and Bullay, the line hugs the right bank of the river and vineyards can be seen climbing steeply on both sides of the water.

Bullay is quaint village. Here the line crosses the Mosel on a long double-deck truss bridge that carries the local road on the lower level. On the far side the railway passes below Prinzenkopf mountain through the tunnel of the same name. On the far side it clings precariously to a hillside in a vineyard using an unusual Hangviadukt 'hanging bridge' which is really a level ledge built to carry the line through this difficult terrain. After passing through another tunnel, the line strays well away from the river which it doesn't rejoin until reaching Trier 115 miles (185 km) upriver from Koblenz. This historic Roman city serves both as a regional railway hub and an important commercial destination in its own right. Those wishing to continue along the river may go on to Luxembourg, where the Mosel forms the border between Germany and this small EU member state, or alternatively head down the lush Saar valley towards Saarbrücken.

Above: A DB local train glides across the two-level deck-truss across the Mosel at Bullay, Germany. The scenic Mosel valley is characterized by lush and steeply sloped terraced vineyards with castles and churches perched precariously on ledges high above the railway and river.

ELBE RIVER VALLEY

From Dresden to Prague

Brian Solomon

Dresden and Prague are two of central Europe's most fascinating cities. They are, however, hugely different in style. Prague represents one of the best-kept large historic city centres in Europe, featuring wonderfully preserved and elaborate architecture that largely escaped the ravages of 20th-century warfare. Dresden is most famous for its destruction by a firestorm caused by Allied bombing on the night of 13–14 February 1945. It has come to symbolize the wasteful destruction of war, but like the legendary phoenix it has risen from its own ashes to thrive again.

Today Dresden treats visitors to a mix of modern and restored historic architecture, best characterized by the Zwinger Palace whose ruined fire-scarred walls and burnt statues of cherubs seem to represent a Germany ravaged by war. The city straddles the Elbe River, its Altstadt (old town) lies on the left bank and the Neustadt (new town) on the right. Ironically the newer part of the city fared better in the bombing, and thus today the Neustadt features a greater concentration of older buildings. The city is blessed with two fine railway stations; the Hauptbahnhof (main railway station) is near the centre of the Altstadt, while Neustadt has its own station. Both feature classic steel and glass train sheds.

Local and through-trains serving the Elbe valley stop at both Dresden stations. The Dresden S1 'S-bahn' local service runs the German portion of the journey at half-hourly intervals throughout the day, making towns along the way easily accessible as part of a day trip from Dresden. S1 trains terminate at Schöna on the German-Czech border. A faster and better class of service is offered at two-hour intervals by international EuroCity trains to Prague. The advantages of the EuroCity trains include more comfortable seating, better windows, an onboard dining car and faster scheduling – approximately 2

hours 45 minutes for the journey from Dresden Hbf to Prague. Yet EC trains do not permit the visitor to explore the many wonders of the Elbe valley first hand.

South of Dresden, the Elbe winds its way through areas protected by the Nationalpark Sächsische Schweiz (Saxon Switzerland National Park) which are among eastern Germany's most beautiful landscapes. Characterized by its rugged terrain and magnificent and sublime sandstone rock formations, this park is favoured by hikers and nature enthusiasts. Local railway stations at Pirna, Königstein, Bad Schandau and Schöna all serve areas of the park. Located at a picturesque bend in the Elbe, the village of Königstein makes for a pleasant stopover. Above the town rests the Festung Königstein, a 15th-century fortress, while the town itself retains its medieval charm, its terracotta-tiled buildings nestling tightly into the hill side. Church bells toll hourly, and a small ferry chugs across the Elbe to the far bank as a procession of tour boats navigate the river.

More popular is Bad Schandau, located a few miles upriver to the south. This historic spa town lies further from its railway station, so a historic tram ride is an added attraction of stopping here. Beyond, the railway hugs tightly to the shore of the Elbe. The best views are all from the left-hand side of the train. At Schöna, another ferry takes visitors across the river, which at this point forms the border between Germany and the Czech Republic. While Schöna is served only by dead-

Above: A ferry shuttles back and forth across the Elbe between the German village of Schöna and its Czech counterpart Hřensko on the opposite bank. Passengers having just arrived by train from Dresden await the ferry to take them across the river to the Czech Republic.

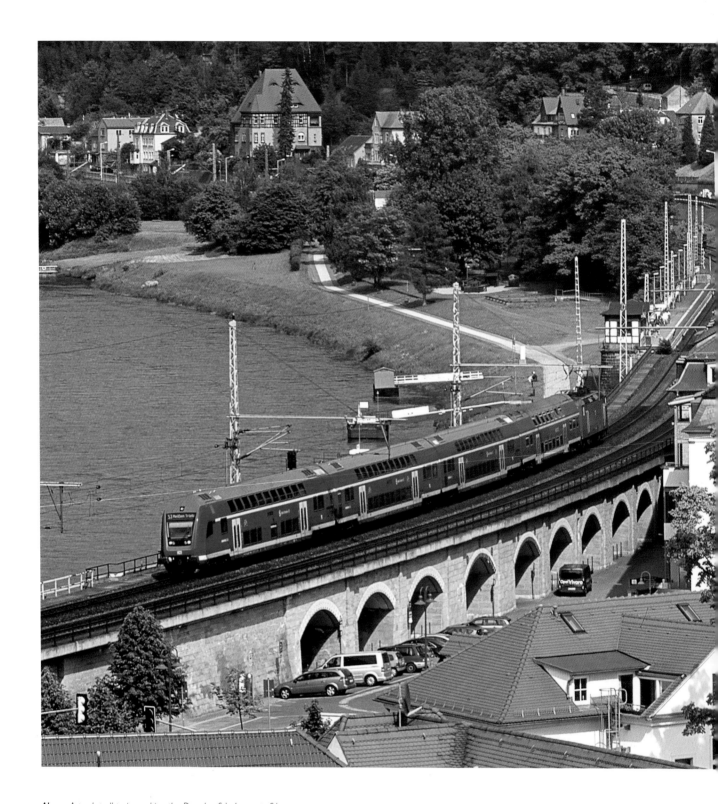

Above: *A push-pull train working the Dresden S-bahn route S1 glides along the viaduct above the Elbe just north of the Königstein station. A public park above the town makes for a pleasant way to spend the afternoon.*

end roads, its Czech counterpart, Hřensko on the right bank, is situated on the main road where its classic architecture is ensconced among unusual cliffs. In Czech the river is called the Labe. Near Děčín, villages are built into the steeply sloped left bank rising high above the railway, and local CD (Czech Railways) trains serve small stations.

Děčín is a big town and an important railway junction, and sits at the confluence of the Labe and Ploučnice Rivers. Most of the town was built on the right side of the Labe, while the main railway station is on the left in the village of Podmokly. A prominent landmark is Děčín medieval fortress which perches picturesquely on cliffs above the river. A wooden structure occupied this site until the 13th century; the present castle was substantially modified in the 16th and 18th centuries. Today, it is a popular attraction. Beyond Děčín, trains use lines on both sides of the river, with the primary intercity route remaining on the left bank. The Labe valley opens up to the south. Through EuroCity trains to Prague run via Ustí nad Labem and Lovosice. Arrival in the Czech capital is at the fittingly impressive art nouveau Prague Main Station (Praha hlavní nádraží) that features a glass-covered steel train shed and intricately decorated station buildings. Don't forget to inspect the numerous carved stone faces on the outside of the station before you venture into Prague to savour the delights of one of Europe's great cities.

Right: Along the railway through the Elbe Valley are several historic villages, including Königstein, nestled tightly between the hills and the west bank of the river.

GERMANY'S HARZER SCHMALSPURBAHNEN

The Harz Mountain Narrow Gauge

Brian Solomon

Germany's Harz Mountains region, popular with tourists for its exceptional scenic beauty and quaint medieval towns, is famous both for romantic legends of witches and for its unusual railway system. Romantic literary master Johann Wolfgang von Goethe was fascinated by the Teutonic lore of Brocken mountain (the highest peak in the Harz range) and incorporated it into his neo-Gothic interpretation of the Faust legend. Goethe died in 1832, but it was another half-century before the narrow-gauge railway was conceived, making this railway a relative late-comer to the region. Today's network originated in two separate systems largely constructed during the 1880s and 1890s, and only connected in 1905. The decentralized nature of the railway reflects this development.

The Harz Mountains region was awkwardly situated on the postwar militarized border between East and West Germany resulting in many areas being off-limits during the tensions of the Cold War era. Yet the Deutsche Demokratische Republik's (DDR) constrained economic climate paradoxically ensured the survival of this narrow-gauge railway as part of the national Deutsche Reichsbahn network. It was the most extensive of eastern Germany's seven surviving narrow-gauge railways, but lack of investment meant that it continued to operate steam locomotives decades after most lines in the West had been either electrified or converted to diesel operation. The DDR's unravelling in 1989 resulted in German reunification in 1990, and re-consolidation of the German railway network. At that time, the Harz Mountain lines were pruned from the national system and set up as a private

Opposite above: Panoramic views from the top of Brocken mountain. A descending HSB excursion spirals down from the summit.

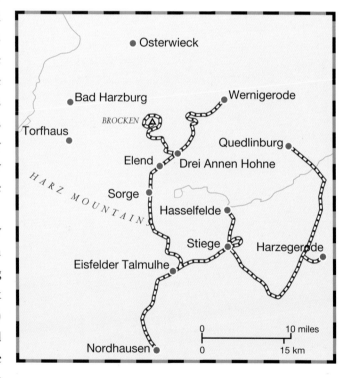

Opposite below: The combination of pleasant mountain scenery, historic steam-hauled trains, Faustian legends and medieval villages makes the Harz Mountains a popular destination year round.

railway under the name Harzer Schmalspurbahnen GmbH (HSB). By that time the continued operation of steam locomotives was viewed as a virtue that would attract tourists, rather than as a burdensome obsolescence, so steam operation was not only retained, but in some instances expanded. Steam operations are maintained year round.

Although popular with visitors, the 87-mile (140-km) HSB is far more than simply a tourist railway. It functions as a key part of the region's transport network. Although as many as ten steam locomotives may work daily, diesel-powered trains and self-propelled railcars augment steam services. Significantly the narrow-gauge railway interfaces with the national railway network operated by Deutsche Bahn at three locations – Nordhausen, Quedlinburg and Wernigerode. In addition, a short portion of its line is shared with Nordhausen's tram network, making for an unusual, but delightful, example of German attitudes towards multi-modal infrastructural flexibility.

There are three distinct portions of the HSB, reflecting both the line's history and contemporary timetables, although services connect various points on the system and cross-platform transfers allow for easy changes between trains. The Harzquerbahn is the primary north-south line running for 38 miles (61 km) to connect the industrial centre of Nordhausen with the popular medieval town of Wernigerode. Drei Annen Hohne (1771 feet/540 m above sea level) is a largely wooded mountain oasis centred on a beautifully restored station located 29 miles (46 km) north of Nordhausen.

Just to the south of Drei Annen Hohne station, the famous Brockenbahn diverges from the Harzquerbahn. This steeply graded line spirals its way up to Brocken (3704 feet/1129 m above sea level). In summer, this is the most intensively steam-operated portion of the railway. But all year round HSB's immaculately maintained 2-10-2T locomotives march steadily up and down the mountain bringing an unending parade of visitors with them. The 3.3 per cent climb (three feet four inches are gained in height for every hundred feet travelled) would be just a nominal climb on a highway, but it exacts a considerable price from the locomotives, which must stop mid-journey at Schierke to take on more water for the boiler. The climb, most of which takes place in thick forest, is accomplished at an exacting, yet leisurely, pace. As the line gains elevation, gaps in the trees hint at the vistas to be enjoyed at the summit. Brocken is the highest peak in the Harz, and the top

Above: The classic station at Drei Annen Hohne is an operations centre and the point where many passengers change trains for the Brockenbahn which winds its way to the top of Brocken mountain. It is one of several well-preserved station buildings along the HSB.

is above the tree line. At the top, passengers are greeted with awe-inspiring panoramic views. Visitors should bring a jacket, even in summer, as fierce winds scour the top of mountain year-round. During the Cold War years, facilities at Brocken served as a Soviet listening post on the West, and these Spartan buildings are a legacy of the uninspired architecture left by the communist regime.

The third portion of the HSB network is too often neglected by visitors. The Selketalbahn joins with the Harzquerbahn at Eisfelder Talmühle using the network's most steeply graded line. This route connects Eisfelder Talmühle with Gernrode and Quedlinburg, along with short branches to Hasselfelde and Harzgerode. Quedlinburg is a UNESCO World Heritage site and is a favourite destination for tourists because of its medieval architecture set amid a maze-like warren of streets. Scenery at this end of the network is more pastoral than the thick forests further west. Steam operations are focused on the Gernrode end of the Selketalbahn, while most through-trains to Eisfelder Talmühle are diesel-powered.

Historical steam-hauled trains traversing scenery ranging from stunning to pastoral over a decentralized network connecting myriad historic towns makes the HSB a joy to explore. It seems that there is a pleasant surprise to be discovered with every new station visited.

Above: HSB's steeply graded narrow-gauge railway requires specialized locomotives. The most common are 2-10-2T steam locomotives which feature low driving wheels for great power at low speeds. One of HSB's perfectly maintained 2-10-2Ts takes water at Drei Annen Hohne before continuing on the next stage of its mountain journey.

ZUGSPITZBAHN

To the Top of Germany

Brian Solomon

The Bayerische Zugspitzbahn (Bavarian Zugspitze Railway) is a tourist railway in the purest sense of the meaning; it was built between 1928 and 1930 to bring day trippers and skiers to the top of Germany's tallest mountain – the Zugspitze which stands 9,718 feet (2,962 m) above sea level on the border between Germany and Austria in southern Bavaria. This exciting railway is among the most interesting German lines offering magnificent mountain views all year round. It is enormously popular, carrying upwards of 600 people per hour at peak travel times.

Germany and its neighbours remain some of the most railway-friendly nations in the western world, and so travelling by train simply to ride the train is not a problem. The Zugspitzbahn begins at Garmisch-Partenkirchen, and there are hourly through-services from Munich on Germany's national network run by DB. Most of these trains run to Mittenwald, just beyond Garmisch, and roughly every second train continues as a through-service to Innsbruck operated in conjunction with ÖBB (Austrian Railways). This makes visiting the Zugspitze an easy day trip from towns in Bavaria and western Austria. Likewise it is easy to tie this journey into a trip to the Austrian or Swiss Alps. In fact, a round trip is easily accomplished, but is best enjoyed over several days, rather than as one rushed adventure.

The Bayerische Zugspitzbahn is a narrow-gauge line with its own Garmisch station found adjacent to DB's. Since it is a separate railway, it has its own fares and tickets – and while this initially may seem comparatively expensive for an hour-long 12-mile (19-km) one-way journey, it is really good value. The journey is completed in stages that reflect different parts of the system and the rugged nature of the scenery. You board the narrow-gauge electric train at Garmisch and climb through the high Alpine valley. Here the line ascends at 3.5 per cent

Opposite: Approaching Eibsee, a Zugspitzbahn rack train descends the steeply graded line from the mountain summit. This is one of the steepest lines in Germany.

(3½ feet rise for every 100 feet travelled) – steep for a mainline railway but gentle compared with the precipitous ascent ahead. A station at Kreuzeck allows for connections with two aerial cable car lines, known respectively as the Kreuzeckbahn and Alpspitzbahn. The first stage of the journey ends at Grainau, the location of the railway's shops, where you change from a conventionally propelled railway car to a rack-railway car that ascends gradients up 14 per cent, too steep for a conventional adhesion railway, which is why the cog-wheel system is used.

Beyond the station at Eibsee (3,307 feet/1,008 m above sea level) the line begins its really tough climb. The line hugs the north face of the mountain, which looms majestically above the valley on the left. Eibsee lake is visible to the right. At Eibsee station there is connection to a direct cable car that goes right to the top of the Zugspitze. For a more interesting journey, stay on the train. Now the line climbs very sharply, reaching an astounding 25 per cent gradient in places. You'll hear the rack dig in, clattering as each cog lifts the train forwards. Having merely hugged the mountainside until now, the railway now aims skyward, climbing well above the tree-line. After a little while, the railway burrows into the mountain entering the Riffelriss Tunnel, as it maintains its steep ascent. Not only is this tunnel among the steepest on any railway, but it features a passing siding. There, in the very bowels of the mountain, your train will pause for one coming the

Below: The Zugspitzbahn operates a range of equipment including some vehicles dating to the 1950s. All vehicles are maintained to very high standards.

other way. The line reaches its terminus at Sonn Alpin, where you change for Gletscherbahn cable car that goes to the top.

The panoramic views from the summit are without parallel. On a clear day you can see all the way to Munich to the north, and south to the Austrian Alps. Once you've taken in the views, you have a choice of return routes. Many travel down the mountain on skis. However, you can return the way you came, or sample the Eibseeseilbahn, the cable car that hangs down the rocky raw north face of the mountain rejoining the railway at Eibsee station. Having made a round trip, you can explore the railway's stations or retrace your route back to Garmisch. The connecting mountain lines that skirt the German-Austrian border offer a range of views and make for interesting additional excursions. You can return to Munich via branches going to Reutte in Tyrol and Kempten. This requires a change of trains at both stations, and while this takes longer, the journey is as much about the sheer enjoyment of travelling as simply getting to the destination. Sit back and watch the snow-crested peaks scrape an azure sky against a rolling backdrop of evergreens. It's majestic.

Above: The Bayerische Zugspitzbahn terminus at Garmisch-Partenkirchen is scenically situated just a short walk from the DB station. The Zugspitzbahn is a narrow-gauge operation; the distance between rail-heads is 3 ft 3³/₄ in (1,000 mm), compared with 4 ft 8¹/₂ in (1,453 mm) standard gauge common to most European lines.

SWISS ALPINE NARROW GAUGE

Remarkable Engineering over the Spine of the Alps

Brian Solomon

No country loves its railways as much as Switzerland. And, perhaps no other nation is better known, or better respected, for its railways. Using spiral tunnels, rack railways, curved viaducts and other creative infrastructure the Swiss built railways in places where one would not dare to install a road. Furthermore, despite terrific Alpine snowfall and exceptionally steep grades, Swiss railways operate with clocklike perfection.

Opposite: A short locomotive-hauled local train crosses a snowy Alpine meadow near Davos Wolfgang. Rhätische Bahn manages to operate a full range of services, including expresses, freight and stopping locals on a single track line across rugged Alpine territory, often in difficult winter weather, and yet maintains a tight schedule.

Matterhorn-Gotthard Bahn

To see Switzerland's mountains at their best you need to travel from west to east since the main north–south routes tend to travel under the mountains rather than across them. There is no better west–east axis than the network of narrow-gauge lines operated by the Matterhorn-Gotthard Bahn and Rhätische Bahn systems, a route most famous for the *Glacier Express*. Travellers on these lines can expect superlative engineering, stellar views and outstanding railway experiences. Since there are a variety of lines available, there is no single best way to approach a narrow-gauge Alpine journey, although the *Glacier Express* and *Bernina Express* are the most popular options.

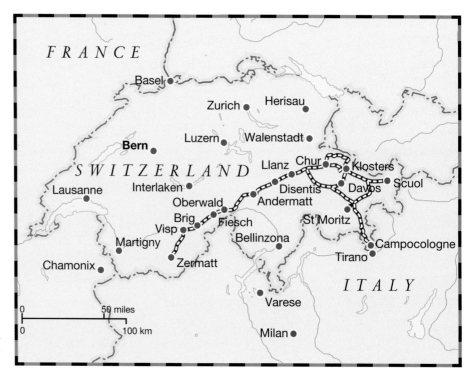

The western end of this network is operated by the Matterhorn-Gotthard Bahn (created in 2003 through the consolidation of the BVZ Zermatt-Bahn and the Furka Oberalp Bahn). The MGB journey involves a series of steep Alpine descents and ascents. On mere mortal railways a gradient of 2 per cent is considered steep, but on the MGB the grades reach 11 per cent on mainlines and are even steeper on branches! The gradients exceed the practicality of normal wheel-to-rail adhesion, so the railway uses the Abt rack system on its steepest grades. The rack is only necessary for especially steep sections and is engaged at speed. A clattering from below the floor is an indication that the train is in rack territory. MGB begins and ends at relatively high elevations, yet, as impressive as this railway is, it is outdone by connecting lines from the word go. At its western end, the MGB terminates high in the Alps at Zermatt. From here the Gornagrat Bahn offers a stunning, albeit expensive, side trip further up the mountains to a perch 10,235 feet (3,120 m) above sea level that is famous for its views of the Matterhorn. This involves a 20 per cent grade, almost twice as steep as MGB's mainline.

The *Glacier Express* begins its eastward journey at Zermatt, and drops down through impressive Alpine terrain, then runs across a broad valley through Visp to Brig. From near Visp passengers will see to the north the route of Bern-Lötschberg-Simplon's old line climbing on a shelf towards the old Lötschberg Tunnel. (A few years ago, BLS's new base tunnel augmented the traditional line.) At Brig MGB's narrow-gauge line stops in front of the BLS station allowing an easy transfer to standard-gauge mainline trains, making this a popular way to reach the narrow gauge from elsewhere in Europe.

East of Brig the MGB climbs sharply. The rack is engaged to bring trains up through a spiral tunnel, which upon exiting the east portal allows a brief glimpse down on the route travelled. The line continues to climb towards the Furka Pass. Above Fiesch, forest gives way to a more barren Alpine setting, which is best appreciated in mid-winter when a thick blanket of snow covers the ground. This portion of the line was largely completed in 1926. However, the original 7,093-feet (2,162-m) crossing of the Furka Pass was only opened in warmer seasons, while in winter tracks were lifted across avalanche zones. This older route ceased to function as the mainline in 1982 when the new 9.5-mile (15.4-km) Furka-

Left: With the hum of electric motors, an immaculate electric Furka-Oberalp train arrives at Fiesch. The F-O Bahn was merged with BVZ Zermatt-Bahn in 2003 forming the Matterhorn-Gotthard Bahn.

Basistunnel (Furka Base Tunnel) opened, which lowered the crossing to 5,131 feet (1,564 m). A portion of the old Furka Pass crossing is now operated as a seasonal preserved line.

MGB's narrow-gauge station at Andermatt rests in the saddle of the Gotthard Pass, much higher than, but nearly directly above, Swiss Federal Railway's (SBB) standard-gauge Gotthard Tunnel. Connecting Andermatt and SBB's station at Göschenen is a truly wild 2.5-mile (4-km) narrow-gauge branch that descends on a phenomenally steep 17.9 per cent grade that drops dramatically through a series of snow sheds and tunnels making for a memorable, if not exceptionally scenic, short railway journey.

Looking east from Andermatt, you can watch a train ascend the Oberalp Pass – 6,667 feet (2,032 m) above sea level – as it swings through a series of ladder-like horseshoe curves. Perhaps even more impressive than watching the train is actually riding it. The view back down to Andermatt makes it look like a model railway scene, which gradually grows smaller as the train gains elevation. Once over the Oberalp Pass the line continues to Disentis, where the MGB meets the Rhätische Bahn – operator of the eastern portion of the narrow-gauge network. *Glacier Express* and other priority trains run through directly from one line to the next without passengers needing to change.

Below: Even in mid-summer, snow-crested peaks may be found in Switzerland. A Rhätische Bahn express ascending the Albula Gorge approaches Preda having wound through twists and spirals on the climb up from Bergün.

Rhätische Bahn

Rhätische Bahn's mainline runs from Disentis to Reichenau-Tamins, where its lines diverge: one route continues towards Chur, the other towards the Albula Gorge and St Moritz. The arrangement of this junction requires trains continuing towards the Albula Gorge to first head into Chur to reverse direction. Chur is the capital of Switzerland's Graubünden canton and is a city of considerable historic significance having been the site of civilized habitation for nearly 5,000 years, as well as now being a railway hub. Rhätische Bahn has a yard here, and this is the beginning of the branch to Arosa, which runs through city streets on its way out of town. At Chur passengers can change to SBB through-trains, or continue on RhB's line northwards that runs parallel to SBB's standard-gauge tracks to Landquart, and then beyond to Klosters where the lines diverge again. One line goes to Davos and continues southwards to Filisur (on the Albula route); the other is the Vereina Line which transits the world's longest narrow-gauge railway mountain tunnel (11.9 miles/19.1 km long and opened on 19 November 1999) to Sagliains (on the line to Scuol). The Swiss enthusiasm for investing in rail travel has led to the construction of this new railway tunnel rather than an Alpine motorway. Like other long Alpine tunnels, it handles car-ferry trains that allow motorists to take a short cut beneath the mountains.

Below: Rhätische Bahn's brilliant red trains complement the cottonwool-like winter landscape at Davos Wolfgang. In addition to a wonderfully punctual service, RhB maintains classically tidy stations at many locations.

Above: *Both* Bernina *and* Glacier Expresses *share the route through the Albula Gorge. Here, an uphill train works the loops near Bergün.*

One of the main differences between MGB and Rhätische Bahn routes is that the RhB relies exclusively on adhesion, and operates the world's steepest lines without the benefit of racks. All of Rhätische Bahn's routes are blessed with exceptional vistas, but its route through the Albula Gorge and over the Bernina Pass permits an experience of one of the greatest railways ever constructed, offering not just spectacular mountain scenery, but especially clever railway engineering. One of the scenic highlights comes beyond Thusis, where the line transits the Schyn Ravine, made famous by J.M.W. Turner's paintings. Another highlight is the Landwasser Viaduct, one of the most photographed railway bridges in the world. This sharply curved stone arch bridge crosses 230 feet (70 m) above the Landwasser River on six semicircular spans, the last of which rests on the side of a tremendous vertical precipice, where the line enters directly into a tunnel on the cliffside.

Just beyond is Filisur station (the junction with the line from Davos), where passengers interested in getting better views of the bridge in snow-free months can get off the train and follow established hiking trails back into the gorge. From an engineering perspective, the most intriguing part of the run is the circuitous stretch in the Albula Gorge between Bergün to Preda where the lines ascends 1,368 feet (417 m) in just 3.75 air-miles (6 km), requiring a steeply graded serpentine route that travels 7.75 rail-miles (12.5 km). This winding track arrangement opened in 1904, and it climbs at 3.5 per cent through a series of spiral tunnels and across tall curved stone viaducts that complete three full loops that overlap one another on a map. This complex arrangement can disorient travellers and even perplex a keen-minded railway enthusiast with a detailed map in hand! At Preda the line ducks into the mountain using the 3.75-mile (6-km) long Albula Tunnel that crests 6,000 feet (1,830 m) above sea level.

This Swiss narrow-gauge network is the highest through-railway in Europe. Beyond is the Bernina Line that reaches the posh ski resort of St Moritz, and connects beyond to Tirano located near the Swiss-Italian frontier. Built between 1908 and 1910, this section crosses its namesake pass, cresting at 7,400 feet (2,255 m) above sea level, then descends some 6,000 feet (1,830 m) through the Poschiavo Valley using a line with maximum gradient of 7.1 per cent. At Tirano passengers can connect with Italian standard-gauge railways.

Having concluded one of the most stunning overland journeys in the world, where the scenery seems to reach from beyond and grab you, it will be difficult to pick a favourite from the procession of magnificent panoramas encountered.

ALPINE PHOENIX

The Furka Cogwheel Steam Railway

Fred Matthews

In August 2010, high in the Alps, one of the most ambitious of all railway restorations came to completion after a quarter-century of volunteer effort and private donations. The Dampfbahn Furka Bergstrecke (Furka Cogwheel Steam Railway) opened the last three miles (4.8 km) of its 11-mile (17.7-km) metre-gauge line over the 6,960-foot (2,121-m) Furka Pass. This line had been closed when, in 1982, the predecessor Furka Oberalp Bahn (now part of the Matterhorn-Gotthard, route of the *Glacier Express*) opened a 9.2-mile (14.8-km) Base Tunnel from Oberwald to Realp, eliminating the need for the rack and permitting all-year operation of this important route. Previously, from the time of its public opening in 1926, the line was usable only from mid-June to early October due to heavy snows and the risk of avalanches during the rest of the year. The celebrated 'folding' Steffenbach bridge was removed and stored for almost eight months of each year.

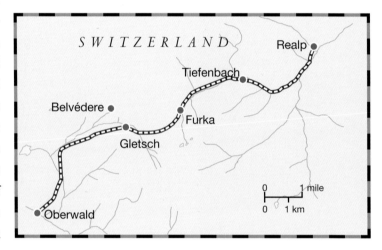

Beginning in the early 1980s, determined volunteer groups got together to raise money and rebuild the line. From 1992, the line reopened in sections west from Realp. Amazingly it began operations with its own original locomotives, handsome 2-6-0 tanks built at Winterthur in 1913–14. These had gone to Vietnam after the Furka Oberalp Bahn electrified in 1941 and were now reclaimed from the jungle.

In contrast to the new Base Tunnel, which allows Realp–Oberwald trains to take a mere 19–25 minutes for the journey, steam trains over the summit take a leisurely 2 hours 20 minutes, punctuated by stops to take on water and allow photo and coffee breaks and short strolls. The gutsy engines march deliberately up the rack, soon climbing above the tree line into wild open country, backed by peaks soaring over 10,000 feet (3,000 m) high. After passing through the 1-mile-long (1.6-km) summit tunnel, the line drops sharply, at up to 11 per cent, past

the much-diminished Rhone Glacier. After a pause at Gletsch, where there are mountain hotels dating from the 1920s, some trains proceed around the underground loop and down the hillside to Oberwald. An 'ultimate' experience for rail and Alpine enthusiasts.

Earlier summers may soon extend the DFB's season a little and more customers may be attracted, since they can make one-way trips. It's useful to check the informative website, www.dfb.ch, for schedules, fares, reservations and the opportunity to assist financially to maintain this breathtaking route.

Above: A DFB train has come over the Furka Pass from Realp, and past the Rhone Glacier (seen here above the train) to arrive in the village of Gletsch (Glacier). Engine 9, a 2-6-0 tank, built by SLM in Winterthur in 1914 for this line, spent 40 years in Vietnam before being reclaimed.

THROAT OF EUROPE

The Gotthard Railway from Open Windows to Tilting Luxury

Fred Matthews

Arguably no other railway in the world combines so many appealing qualities as the mountain section of Switzerland's Gotthardbahn, from the junction of Arth-Goldau southeast of Lucerne, up the Reuss valley, over the 3,786-foot (1,154-m) summit, inside the 9¼-mile (15-km) peak tunnel, then down through the Ticino valley to another major junction at Bellinzona. In the intervening 67 miles (108 km) trains pass many awe-inspiring jagged Alpine peaks that soar up to 10,000 feet (3,000 m) high. Until the era of air-conditioning, passengers in their droves used to hang out of the train windows to obtain the full experience.

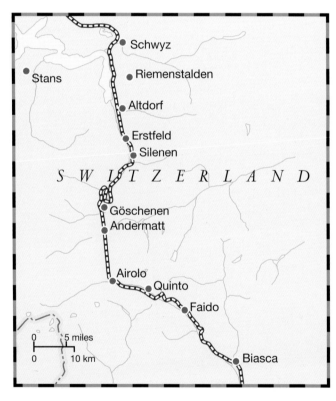

Apart from the exhilarating scenery, the most celebrated aspects of the journey are the loops, or spirals, by which the ruling 2.6 per cent (1 in 41) grade was maintained. The most famous of these are over the north ramp, at Wassen, where the bright little church appears from the train at three different angles as it circles to gain elevation. There are four loops on the south ramp, two below Rodi-Fiesso and a stacked pair between Lavorgo and Giornico. Giornico is also famed for its Romanesque churches, the highest concentration of these imposing 12th century structures found along the Ticino River. Unlike central Switzerland, where most churches were rebuilt in the Baroque style in the 17th century, impoverished Ticino retained its medieval places of worship.

Train services are intensive. In daytime hours there are two passenger trains per hour each way over the steep ramps from Erstfeld, 20 miles (32 km) south of Arth-Goldau, to Biasca, 12 miles (19 km) north of Bellinzona. The journey takes between 1½ and 2 hours depending on whether the train is 'nonstop' or not. Two or three freight trains per hour run in each direction on the busier days of

Opposite: Half the fun was leaning out. An express from Milan to the north begins the dizzying double loops in the Ticino River canyon between Giornico and Lavorgo. The baggage car six back indicates that the train will divide at Arth-Goldau, half for Zurich, half for Basle and the north.

the week (Tuesday to Saturday). After midnight freights move freely; many trains run for morning arrivals.

From its beginning, the Gotthard Railway has had political significance – necessarily so, given the importance of this central trade route. As railways developed, a central Alpine crossing became essential to Germany, Italy and Switzerland. After years of negotiation about routes, a Gotthard treaty was signed by the newly unified governments in 1871, decreeing strict equality of access. Construction was a gargantuan task and killed many workers but on final completion in 1882 it transformed international travel – as revealed by Henry James's novel *Roderick Hudson*, set around 1870, in which he describes passengers having to walk up the steeper grades behind the coach.

Studies for electrification began soon after 1900. Given the line's tunnels and steep grades, this was the first target in what became, after the First World War fuel shortages, an official plan to electrify the entire Swiss rail system over 40 years. Construction began in 1918; power on the ramps went on in late 1920, though a locomotive shortage forced joint steam-electric operation for a few years. Clearly proud of its history, the SBB maintains a handful of the last Gotthard steam engines, the C5/6 2-10-0s built from 1913 to 1917, one or two of which are available for special service.

The Gotthard line's future is as political as were its origins. After years of disputation between Berne and Brussels over the 'need' for more road space through the Alps, Swiss citizens voted to limit truck traffic and build a 35-mile (56-km) Base Tunnel under the entire mountain section, between points near Erstfeld and Biasca. The principal goal of the Base Tunnel is to increase freight capacity to relieve the roads but Zurich–Milan rail passengers will save 45 minutes on their journeys. The old mountain line will remain for some lighter freights plus an hourly tourist train calling at the remaining open station. Through passenger services will be operated by new 150-mph (240-km/h) luxury tilting trains, replacing the ETR 470s, which have run from the late 1990s. So, even after 2016 the Gotthard's hourly mountain trains will still offer one of the greatest loop-the-loop experiences in world railroading.

Opposite above: At Göschenen in 1963, seen from a northbound express, a southbound is ready to go into the Summit Tunnel while a car-carrier waits to follow it. The iconic Ae6/6 electrics (worthy successors of the C5/6 steamers) are disappearing in 2011 after 56 years of service.

Above: Epitome of steam on the Gotthard Pass: one of the C5/6 Class compound 2-10-0s built by SLM in 1914-17. They worked on other lines into the 1960s. At Delemont, Basel–Lausanne line, a special pauses in 1997.

Opposite below: Göschenen in 2000. Sealed windows, greater speed and comfort: an Italian-built ETR 470 Cisalpino tilting train accelerates out of the tunnel.

AUSTRIAN ALPINE CROSSING

Four Alpine Passes

Brian Solomon

Austria's intercity network, operated by ÖBB (Österreichische Bundesbahnen), owes most of its route structure to lines constructed to serve the old Austro-Hungarian Empire before the First World War. The principal standard-gauge routes include four major Alpine crossings, known for their movement of heavy freight and passenger traffic. The Brenner, Tauern and Semmering Passes are on north–south alignments, while the Arlberg Pass is on an east–west alignment. All four routes remain important despite the political changes and redefining of international boundaries that have occurred as a result of the two world wars. Steep gradients, tall bridges, tunnels and spectacular Alpine scenery make these routes among the most interesting main lines in central Europe, while the high quality of ÖBB intercity trains make them a joy to travel upon. In general, travel by intercity trains across Austria is an immensely civilized experience. Such journeys are enjoyable at all times of the year, but are

Opposite: The Arlberg is Austria's east-west link via Switzerland. In addition to long-distance EuroCity services between Vienna and Zürich, local trains serve small stations west of Innsbruck. A push-pull local set works near Flaurling.

most impressive in winter when snow blanketing the Alpine slopes adds an extra dimension of awe, best experienced from the comfort and safety of a passenger carriage with large plate-glass windows.

Arlberg Pass

Austria's Westbahn was built under the direction of Julius Lott in the 1880s. Its most difficult engineering challenge was to get over the Arlberg Pass, a rocky cleft that represents a longitudinal trough in the western Austrian Alps. Railway lines converge at Feldkirch in the western corner of the Austrian Vorarlberg for the ascent of the pass. One route comes from Switzerland, and

Above: A Taurus electric locomotive leads an ÖBB EuroCity express train from Vienna and Innsbruck westward across the Trianna Gorge. The river winds below in the shadows while Schloss Weisberg looms above the line.

skirts through Liechtenstein. Another angles down from the shores of Lake Constance where it connects with lines to Germany. Most through-passenger-trains use the Swiss route from Zürich. The line crests the summit within the 6.37-mile (10.25-km) long Arlberg Tunnel – a bore completed in 1884. Train riders may relax within the long bore, a far superior passage beneath the Alps than the equivalent claustrophobic trip by car through the parallel 8.7-mile (13.98-km) long road tunnel that was completed in 1978.

Exiting the Arlberg Tunnel, the line passes popular ski resorts near St Anton am Arlberg as the track begins its spectacular descent towards Innsbruck following the course of the Rosanna River. At Wiesberg, the line crosses Trianna Viaduct by means of an immense bow-string arch over narrow Trianna Gorge. The bridge sits in the shadow of Schloss Weisberg making for one of the most spectacular railway settings in Europe. Beyond that, the line descends through the town of Landeck. On the right-hand side of the train, the view across the valley discloses castles clinging precipitously to cliff sides. East from Landeck, the line follows the River Inn through a broadening valley that gradually drops towards Innsbruck.

As the railway nears the city, riders on the left-hand side will see another line ascending the mountain to the south. This line connects at Innsbruck, and offers another stunning journey as it crosses the border into Germany. Trains run to the Bavarian resort town of Garmisch, where connections can be made to the amazing Zugspitzbahn (see page 94) and beyond to Munich. Connections at Innsbruck can also be made with trains travelling south over the Brenner Pass to Italy, and east through Austria to Salzburg, Linz and Vienna. Innsbruck is the capital of the Tyrol, and is one of the finer Austrian cities featuring many ornately decorated buildings. With the spine of the Alps rising to the south above the waiting trains, the Innsbruck Hauptbahnhof features the most stunning backdrop of any big railway terminal in Europe.

Brenner Pass

Running southwards from Innsbruck, the route over the Brenner Pass is among the oldest Alpine trade routes in central Europe and was the location of an old Roman road. The railway over the pass, built to connect Innsbruck with Verona (Italy), was completed in 1867. This has developed into one of Europe's busiest mountain freight routes. To simplify freight moves, an avoiding line around Innsbruck was completed in 1994 as part of a greater scheme to increase Austrian railway capacity which includes additional freight bypass lines and construction of a long base-tunnel. Ferry-trains over the pass are operated from a terminal near Wörgl and operate at regular intervals during the day. It is cheaper to transport trucks by rail over the Brenner than to pay the tolls on the adjacent motorway. The avoiding line navigates a long tunnel joining the mainline from

Below: Although less remarked than its Austrian counterpart, the Italian side of the Brenner Pass has its attractions. An FS (Italian State Railways) express train glides through an Alpine valley against the backdrop of stately Castel Pietra fortress.

Innsbruck at Gärberbach in the confines of the narrow gorge of the River Sill. The junction is easy to miss, but can be seen from the left side of the train. Passengers may notice a steady procession of freights as their train ascends the pass. It is common for express passenger trains to overtake freights waiting in passing sidings. The station at Matrei has sidings for trains in both directions. The village is located just a short walk south of the station and features several classic Gasthausen (guest houses) that make it a pleasant point to stop over on a long journey.

The line climbs steeply beyond Matrei. At St Jodok, it makes a tight horseshoe curve, a portion of which is in a tunnel, as it loops around the village gaining elevation towards the top of the pass. Here the best vistas are from the right-hand side of the train, and it is possible to look back down the Sill valley as the train approaches the top of the horseshoe. The line winds through a more forested area as it reaches the top of the Brenner, passing another short tunnel north of Ritten before reaching the summit. The top of the pass is a saddle in the mountains at 4,501 feet (1,372 m) above sea level and it marks the border between Austria and Italy. The border was moved northwards to this location at the end of the First World War, when Austria ceded south Tyrol to Italy.

The Brenner Pass – known in Italian as Passo del Brennero and Brenner Sattel in German – lies at the significant divide between the Adriatic and Black Sea watersheds. Historically all trains changed locomotives here because of the different national railway systems and differences in electrification. ÖBB uses high-voltage alternating current, while FS (Italian State Railway) uses direct current. However, today modern multi-voltage locomotives and changes in railway policy mandated by the EU enable some locomotives to run through unchanged.

Immediately south of the border the line begins its descent into Italy. A modern line relocation has reduced curvature, and made this side of the pass less spectacular than it used to be historically. When the line rejoins its older alignment, it passes several interesting towns, affording views of historic castles and other fortifications. While the scenery is not as lush as on the Austrian side of the pass, the stark drop through the narrow gorge at Fortezza is especially impressive.

Above: To maintain a steady ascent of the Brenner Pass, the railway makes a sweeping horseshoe curve around the picturesque village at St Jodok. A local train is seen approaching its station stop.

Semmering

The crossing of Austria's Semmering Pass was built as part of the railway conceived in the 1830s to connect the imperial capital at Vienna with the Adriatic port at Trieste (now in Italy). The first part of this route opened in 1839, and it was among the earliest railways in Europe to ascend a major mountain grade. Work on the steepest grade sections began in 1848, and the route was completed in 1854, using a summit tunnel in the saddle of the Semmering Pass. A second tunnel (4,960 feet/1,512 m long), built parallel to the first, opened in 1952. The route was finally electrified in 1959, several years later than the other Austrian Alpine crossings, so for more than a century steam locomotives lifted trains over this difficult mountain line.

Most freights and many passenger trains required 'banking' locomotives at the rear for assistance on the steepest portions of the line. Even today, many freight trains use electric locomotives fore and aft over the summit. Today the Semmering route is among the most heavily travelled mountain lines in central Europe. The volume of freight and passenger traffic and the sinuous, difficult nature of the line has made it a candidate for a 13.7-mile (22-km) long base tunnel which may someday augment or bypass the original Semmering crossing.

Below: The Semmering route opened in 1854, making it among the first European mountain mainlines. It features several massive stone viaducts. At some point, a modern deep base-tunnel may bypass much of this original construction.

The Semmering Pass lies on the main route for through-passenger-trains from Vienna to Graz (and beyond to Slovenia), and to Villach (with international overnight trains continuing to Italy). The most interesting portion of the route is between Gloggnitz and Semmering on the northeast side of the pass. The line follows the River Schwarza eastwards through a picturesque valley to Payerbach. The most interesting view is from the left-hand side of the train, as the line makes a tremendous horseshoe curve beyond the Payerbach station, and so it is possible to see the line on the far side of the valley as one approaches Payerbach, and then to look back over the route travelled after leaving it. Payerbach itself is a quaint Austrian village and provides an interesting interlude for travellers wishing to stop for the night. A seasonal narrow-gauge railway connects with the mainline here. West of the town, the line crosses the Schwarza on an impressive masonry viaduct.

The railway climbs steeply towards Semmering, winding through several tight horseshoe curves and over arched stone viaducts. After passing the Weinzettefled Tunnel, the line levels out briefly at the resort station in Breitenstein. Climbing sharply after Breitenstein, the line passes two more short tunnels before reaching the long bores at Semmering. The descent from the summit toward Mürzzuschlag and beyond to Bruck an der Mur is pleasant, but not as dramatic.

Below: At the village of Breitenstein, the sun gleams through the clouds following a heavy summer rain shower that soaked the north slope of the Semmering Pass. This route enjoys an hourly local service from Vienna as well as luxurious express trains.

Tauern Pass

The last of the major Austrian mountain lines completed was the Tauernbahn which opened over its namesake pass at the turn of the 20th century. This main north–south route connects Salzburg with Villach via Bischofshofen and Schwarzach-St Veit. Historically the route accommodates international through-services connecting Germany and cities in Slovenia, Croatia and Serbia, but today most traffic takes the form of nicely equipped domestic intercity trains that run between Salzburg and Villach at two-hourly intervals during most of the day.

Salzburg is one Austria's most beautiful and famous cities, closely associated with its historical role as a salt-mining centre and with the prodigious classical composer, Wolfgang Mozart. Located on the banks of the Salzach River, it is situated close to the border with Germany at the northern reaches of the Alps. Salzburg is an ideal jumping off point for a trip on the Tauernbahn. Trains run southwards through the scenic Salzach and Gastein valleys.

Badgastein is a famous spa resort, known for its curative mineral baths. Renowned for its springs from as early as the 7th century, Badgastein was developed as an Alpine spa in the 15th century. In the 19th century, high-profile visitors, including the composer Franz Schubert, German Kaiser Wilhelm I and Habsburg nobility, brought the town an international reputation. The arrival of the railway made this popular location more accessible and it grew accordingly. Beyond Badgastein the line crosses the spine of the Alps in the Tauerntunnel.

Beyond the pass, the scenery is stunning. The railway runs on a shelf high above the valley floor with spectacular vistas revealing themselves on the right-hand side. Improvements to the original line in the late 20th century included several short line relocations and the construction of massive new infrastructure as characterized by large concrete arch bridges. A rural junction at Lendorf is where the Tauern line joins with a route to Italy via Lienz. Connecting services to this route can be made at Spittal-Millstättersee. A handful of ÖBB trains from Lienz operate via the Italian town of Fortezza to Innsbruck making a circular trip via the Brenner Pass back to Salzburg possible in a day – albeit a long one. Whenever possible, wise travellers should take advantage of the excellent dining cars on the IC/EC trains.

Above: The Tauern route is the least accessible of Austria's four main Alpine passes. A southward freight glides across the immense concrete arch at Penk on the south slope of the Tauern.

Gliding rapidly through lush valleys, along high shelves carved into mountain-sides, and penetrating the soul of the Alps through long tunnels, all with Teutonic efficiency, makes an Austrian rail journey an exceedingly pleasant experience.

EUROSTAR

London to Paris by Rail

Brian Solomon

One of the great European rail journeys is provided by the streamlined *Eurostar* running at regular intervals to connect London with Paris and Brussels using specially built high-speed lines and the world famous Channel Tunnel. This great feat of engineering was anticipated for nearly two centuries before it was completed. The proximity of Britain to continental Europe and the constant necessity of crossing the English Channel by boat had encouraged generations of engineers and planners to dream of building a tunnel to connect England to France. French engineer Albert Mathieu first proposed the construction of a trans-channel tunnel in 1800, fully a generation before the first public steam railway came into service.

Over the years numerous plans for channel tunnels and bridges were discussed, and tunnel companies were formed. In the 1980s, a serious plan got underway and in May 1994, the tunnel was opened by Britain's Queen Elizabeth II and French president François Mitterrand. International high-speed *Eurostar* services began at the end of the year. Today the Channel Tunnel is one of Europe's most significant pieces of railway infrastructure. It measures 31.4 miles (50.5 km) long, of which 24 miles (38.6 km) are located 147.6 feet (45 m) below the seabed of the English Channel – the body of water that separates Britain from continental Europe.

France's high-speed link to the Channel Tunnel was ready in time for the tunnel's opening, but Britain's took another 14 years to complete. As a result, initially *Eurostar* services worked out of London Waterloo International, with trains running to both Paris and Brussels, and seasonal services to the Swiss Alps. In 2008, the fully modernized St Pancras International opened to allow *Eurostar* to serve the magnificent 1867-built balloon-style iron train shed.

Opposite: Eurostar *trains are an adaptation of the French TGV design. Not only do trains travel at high speeds but they need to operate using a variety of different electrification systems and comply with different countries' signalling requirements.*

The ability to board a high-speed train in London and travel to continental capitals in two hours is one of the great achievements of the age. Normally the journey is so smooth that the wonders of the infrastructure are only appreciated through the convenience and comfort of the journey. Interestingly, one of the best ways to appreciate the achievement of the Channel Tunnel is on the rare occasions when a train is stopped below the Channel because of congestion. The *Eurostar* gets most of the publicity, but it is one of several services that keep the Tunnel busy. Freight trains and car and container lorry ferry-shuttle trains represent the majority of the traffic operating through the tunnel. Two 'crossovers' located in the Tunnel permit trains to cross between mainline tracks. When the *Eurostar* is stopped for a crossover move, passengers may hear dripping water and catch a whiff of the sea, all part of the journey's thrill.

Opposite: The highlights of a Eurostar journey are departing from classic European terminals in a modern train; travelling at 186 mph (300 km/h) in total comfort and safety; and zipping below the English Channel – a journey that Napoleon dreamed of making two centuries ago.

Below: The Channel Tunnel is made of three parallel tubes: two outside bores each carry a single railway track, while a narrower central bore is a service tunnel.

CALEDONIAN SLEEPER

Overnight to the West Highlands

Brian Solomon

Historically, overnight sleeping car trains connected cities across the United Kingdom. As late as the mid 1980s, dozens of trains plied the rails nightly, allowing passengers to use their travel time judiciously while experiencing the thrill of arriving in a new destination in the early morning light. Sadly, most overnight runs have vanished as result of changes in travel patterns. Yet, thanks to sustained public demand, a handful of overnight runs do survive. The *Night Riviera* runs nightly, except for Saturdays, between London Paddington and Penzance in Cornwall. Running north from London Euston are Scot Rail's *Caledonian* sleepers serving myriad destinations in Scotland. Trains to Highlands destinations depart after 9 p.m. in the form of one large train, which then splits into three sections at Edinburgh, heading to Aberdeen, Inverness and Fort William respectively while serving intermediate destinations en route. A later departure provides sleeper service between London, Glasgow and Edinburgh. These overnight survivors are among the most unusual, and most exotic, regularly scheduled trains in the UK, offering a throwback to another era that gives today's travellers the welcome opportunity to experience modern sleeping car travel in style.

The most exciting of these journeys is unquestionably the *Caledonian Sleeper* to Fort William. You begin in the concrete canyons of Euston Station – London's least inspiring mainline terminal – yet are immediately treated to an exceptional modern railway experience. The sleeping car train is comprised of well-adorned 'MkIII' passenger cars, a design noted for its excellent ride quality. Unlike the vast majority of train services on the UK network which are made up of cramped self-propelled trains, the sleeping cars give passengers comfort and quality. A train

Opposite above: The Caledonian Sleeper near Rannoch Moor. Most trains in the UK are self-propelled railcars; but the Caledonian Sleeper is hauled by a General Motors-built class 67 diesel-electric.

Opposite below: Lightly travelled lines in Scotland use a radio-token system to authorize train movements; this ensures only one train at a time occupies the line while obviating the high costs of line-side signal hardware.

attendant meets you on the platform and helps you to settle into your compartment. You are allowed to board well before departure, and by the time the powerful electric locomotive eases the train northwards, you may already be ensconced in the lounge.

The *Caledonian Sleeper* takes prides in promoting regional beverages, and you'll find an unusual selection of Scottish ales and whiskies to choose from. Before long the train is racing along the high-speed West Coast mainline; local stations pass by at speed, leaving little more than an impression of a flash of light and curious glances from suburban travellers waiting on the platforms. By the time you pause at the historic railway crossroads at Crewe, you'll probably be tucked up in bed. In the wee hours, you'll feel a bump and clang as the sleepers are shunted at Edinburgh. By the time you wake in the morning, a diesel – typically a General Motors-built class 67 – will be leading you westwards along the Clyde estuary. The line heads inland, but continues to follow waterways.

Above: In the final evening glow, the daily freight from Fort William descending from Corrour Summit crosses a double intersection Warren truss bridge at Rannoch Moor. Not far behind is the Caledonian Sleeper on its way to London.

At Crianlarich (A' Chrìon Làraich in Scottish Gaelic), there's a junction with the line to Oban. Beyond, the train reaches the most wild and desolate scenery – a stark, yet serenely beautiful landscape that varies with each and every sunrise. Some mornings fog and mists cling to the ground, others are met by a clear sky. The most extraordinary blend mists and sun to create a kaleidoscope of colour and texture. Grassy hills rise above bog lands, a shaft of sun will punctuate the grey of low-lying mist, the train rounds a bend and the landscape magically opens up. Approaching Bridge of Orchy (Drochaid Urchaidh), the line sweeps through a broad horseshoe curve, and on many mornings the train is bathed with its first rays of sun here.

The West Highland Line reached Fort William in 1894, but has always been relatively lightly travelled. Historically train movements were governed by electric train tokens and semaphore signals; today, a modern radio token system protects trains as they travel over the single line. Bridge of Orchy is one of many places where trains may meet. In addition to the *Caledonian Sleeper*, local diesel rail cars, called Sprinters, and the occasional freight ply the line.

As the line climbs into the West Highlands, the scenery gets more impressive. There are few roads on Rannoch Moor (Mòinteach Raineach) and many of the vistas here can only be seen by train or by making long hikes. Rannoch Moor

station, located 1,000 feet (305 m) above sea level, is especially remote. Beyond the platforms, the line crosses a nine-span, double-intersection, Warren truss bridge on its ascent to Corrour (Coire Odhar) Summit. The most impressive scenery is to the left. Corrour station lies at 1,338 feet (408 m) above sea level. The sleeper may pause here and then begin its descent towards Fort William. The line drops along Loch Treig, which on clear mornings appears as a crystalline azure mirror. As the line descends, the scenery becomes more wooded, and between Tulloch and Roy Bridge the line transits the confines of a deep rocky gorge. As the *Sleeper* approaches Fort William, Ben Nevis, the tallest peak in the British Isles, makes its appearance on the left.

Although a stub-end station, Fort William does not mark the end of the West Highland line. In 1901, an extension was built to the fishing port of Mallaig (Malaig). Local trains work this scenically supreme line three or four times daily. The best time to ride is in summer, when one turn is scheduled with a steam locomotive and vintage carriages. Highlights of the trip are views of Ben Nevis, the rugged coast, 11 short tunnels and passage over the curved Glenfinnan Viaduct. Mallaig sits perched above a compact horseshoe-shaped harbour. Ferries connect to the Isle of Skye. This peaceful, rural place seems a whole world away from London where your journey began only a few hours before.

SETTLE TO CARLISLE RAILWAY

England's Most Scenic Mainline

Brian Solomon

Britain's highly acclaimed Settle and Carlisle line made headlines when the old nationalized British Rail tried to trim the route from the network – twice – first in the 1960s, and again in the 1980s. The popularity of the line secured first its survival and then its revival in recent years. Several stations along the line that had been closed during the lean years have been restored and reopened, while the line's infrastructure was renewed and improved. Today, the S&C carries more passengers than it did historically, and for good reasons. It is popular with railway enthusiasts, day trippers, hill-walkers and tourists.

The old BR network was privatized in 1994, and today the S&C route is operated by Northern Rail, which assigns class 156 and 158 diesel rail cars to its Leeds–Settle–Carlisle services. Trains operate every two to three hours. A special 'Settle & Carlisle Day Ranger' ticket is available giving passengers unlimited travel between stations at Skipton and Carlisle, enabling visitors to hop on and off trains at their leisure and to experience highlights of the line by train and by foot.

The S&C was built in the 1870s, the product of the Midland Railway's expansion towards the Scottish border. It was among the last important mainlines constructed in England, and opened in 1876, more than half a century after George Stephenson's Stockton & Darlington had spurred the railway fever that linked virtually every sizeable village in Britain. The route was built primarily to serve express trains and did so at the expense of communities along the line. Rather than build to town centres,

Opposite: Local trains on the Settle & Carlisle use standard diesel multiple units, such as this class 153 seen at Ribblehead station. This station is maintained by the Settle & Carlisle Railway Trust.

Above: The Settle & Carlisle has been a popular route for steam excursions. Here a mainline excursion roars across the Ribblehead Viaduct.

S&C's engineers followed the most efficient profile to minimize gradients but often placed local stations an inconvenient distance from towns. The lack of nearby villages along the central portion of the line accentuates its desolate windswept qualities.

The scenery is characterized by rolling hills with sparse vegetation, a mix of bogland, grasses and moss, but with very few trees or built structures. Rugged terrain demanded a highly engineered line, and the S&C route features 14 tunnels, 325 small bridges and 21 viaducts (defined as a long multi-span bridge). Most of the stations and infrastructure on the line date from its original construction, while the use of traditional upper quadrant semaphore signals to govern train movements adds to its nostalgic appeal. Revenue steam locomotive operation ended in 1968, but over the last four decades the S&C has been a favourite for historic excursions, and many of Britain's most famous locomotives have hauled trains on the line.

The entire line from Settle to Carlisle is noted for its scenic splendour and is dotted with noteworthy infrastructure. The most interesting portion of the route is between Settle and Garsdale where the railway transits the Yorkshire Dales National Park. Settle station opened in 1876, and was just one of three stations serving the line's namesake town. The line runs northwards following the Ribble valley through Stainforth and Helwith Bridge. Horton-in-Ribblesdale is one of several stations closed during the line's nadir (in the 1960s and 1970s) and re-opened in 1986. Beyond Horton, S&C assumes its iconic image crossing windswept pastures and bogs against the backdrop of the Three Peaks of the Yorkshire Dales.

Ribblehead station is near the line's most famous structure, the famed 24-arch Ribblehead Viaduct; measuring 440 yards (402 m), this is the longest bridge on the line and was constructed from an estimated 1.5 million bricks. At Blea Moor, the line crosses a watershed divide in the longest tunnel on the line measuring 2,629 yards (2,404 m). Looming above the tunnel is Ingleborough, which rises 2,372 feet (723 m) and is the second highest of the Three Peaks. Immediately north of Blea Moor Tunnel is the Dent Head Viaduct. Dent station sits at 1,150 feet (350 m) above sea level, making it the highest mainline station in the UK. Beyond Dent, the line crests at Ais Gill (Summit) at 1,169 feet (356 m), then drops steadily as it continues its northward path. The most impressively situated station is at Garsdale, which while slightly lower than Dent, seems to rest on top of the world. S&C's tallest bridge is the magnificent 12-arch limestone Smardale Viaduct that rises 131 feet (40 m) above Scandal Beck.

Enjoy the remainder of the journey to Carlisle as the train passes through the Cumbrian Fells and the pastoral Eden Valley. Alternatively, take a break at one of several intermediate stations to explore the surroundings or make a return journey over one Britain's most loved lines. While scheduled passenger services are relatively infrequent compared with more populated lines in the UK, there are ample trains to allow exploration at various locations. In addition to passenger traffic, the line is a favoured freight corridor for coal and aggregate trains.

Above: Well before privatization, British Rail operated long locomotive-hauled trains on the Settle & Carlisle route. In this view of the Dent Head Viaduct, a BR-painted class 47 and carriages make for a traditional image of the old railway.

WELSH NARROW GAUGE

Historic Mountainous Slate-Hauling Lines

Brian Solomon

The sinuous, meandering narrow-gauge tracks that connect villages and halts in the mountains of north Wales are among the great railway experiences of the British Isles. Here dramatic scenery can be enjoyed at a leisurely pace behind historic steam locomotives that gently work their way along some of the narrowest tracks used by passenger trains anywhere in the world.

The concept of a railway linking slate quarries in north Wales with docks on the Irish Sea had a relatively early beginning, with the first serious proposal being considered in 1832. Unlike mainline British railways that were constructed to the Stephenson Standard gauge of 4 feet 8½ inches (1,435 mm), Welsh slate-hauling lines were built with narrow-gauge tracks and the region is considered the birthplace of the narrow-gauge movement. Construction of the Ffestiniog Railway (spelling variations are the result of Anglicized renderings of Welsh names, and Welsh spellings of English names) began in 1836, and its track gauge was just 23½ inches (597 mm), which was less than half the width used by most mainline railways. The standard had been established in the slate quarries where horse-drawn wagons needed to navigate unusually tight curves. Running from Blaenau Ffestiniog to Porthmadog, this novel railway began as a gravity-operated commodity-specific line. Trainloads of slate were rolled from quarry to waterfront while empty cars were hauled back upgrade by horse.

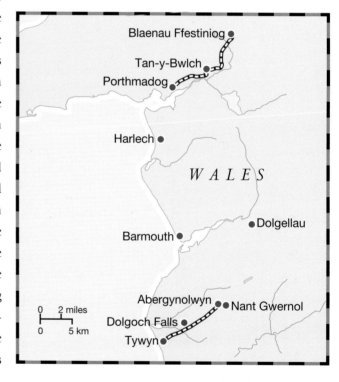

The 1860s saw two significant improvements: introduction of locomotives and passenger services. In the 1870s, Ffestiniog adopted the unusual double-ended Fairlie-type locomotive that was designed for greater haulage on lightweight tracks. These locomotives have become a trademark of the line ever since. The arrival of standard-gauge lines to the slate-producing region simultaneously drew freight traffic away from the narrow gauge while opening the region up to tourism.

Tourist traffic to the Welsh mountains gradually outpaced slate traffic. In the 1920s, the 25-mile (40-km) Welsh Highland Railway was opened from a connection with the Ffestiniog at Porthmadog over the scenic Aberglaslyn Pass to Caernarfon. Despite popularity with visitors, these narrow-gauge lines closed during the Second World War and were not reopened after peace had been declared.

In the early 1950s, public fascination with the Welsh narrow gauge, combined with a desire to attract tourists to the region, led to Britain's earliest historic railway restoration efforts. The preservation of the Talyllyn Railway resulted in what is considered the world's first preserved line setting important precedents both for the development of other Welsh narrow-gauge lines and for further railway preservation across the British Isles. The movement to reopen the Ffestiniog resulted in the operation and ownership of the line passing to a charitable trust. Gradually, through the dedication of railway enthusiasts and preservationists, the railway was rebuilt. Complicating these efforts was construction of a reservoir near the top end of the line which required the construction of a 2-mile (3.2-km) line deviation and a new tunnel.

Today the Ffestiniog Railway is among Britain's foremost preserved railways and it operates a 13½-mile (21.7-km) line between its historic terminals. At

Above: As built, the Ffestiniog line required two tunnels on its line from Blaenau Ffestiniog to Porthmadog. The shorter of these two original tunnels is still in service; an up-bound train led by locomotive Linda nears the west portal during a June downpour.

Blaenau Ffestiniog the railway shares a station with standard-gauge British rail trains (serving the branch line from Llandudno Junction), with further connections available at Minffordd Station. This integration allows the narrow gauge to serve as a seasonal through-route with the British railway network. In addition, the recent reconstruction (during the 1990s and 2000s) of the Welsh Highland Railway (Rheilffordd Eryri) now allows for a nearly 40-mile (64-km) narrow-gauge journey, with a change of trains at Porthmadog.

There's an indescribable thrill boarding the slim-gauge train in the slate-infused environment at Ffestiniog with mountains of waste stone in pyramid-like piles north of the line. As the train clatters leisurely downgrade, you pass the remnants of the once thriving slate quarries, and stone cottages with slate roofs, that seem to have stepped right off the pages of Tolkien's Middle Earth. Before long the line is on the modern-era deviation and the north portal of the old Moelwyn Tunnel is visible from the train. After escaping the inky gloom of the new tunnel – one of the longest built for a preserved railway – you'll wind around the full spiral at Dduallt, which seems like the feature of an oversized model railway. As the line descends, the mountains loom high on the right, while the occasional panorama across the valley can be seen to the left. By Tan-y-Bwlch, the line runs through thickly forested hillsides. The line snakes around to maintain a steady descending gradient. The railway has shops at Boston Lodge, then crosses a long causeway to reach Portmadog.

Above: A Fairlie-type locomotive named David Lloyd George leads a Ffestiniog train up-grade through the modern-era spiral at Dduallt, Wales. Ffestiniog has many charms and remains popular with railway enthusiasts and tourists alike.

Talyllyn Railway

Running 7.3 miles (11.74 km) from Nant Gwernol to Tywyn Wharf, the 2 foot 3 inch gauge (686 mm) Talyllyn got its start in the 1860s. Like the Ffestiniog, it was initially intended for movement of slate, but it opened to passenger traffic soon after it was completed. In the early 20th century it benefited from tourist interest, yet continued to thrive primarily on the slate business. The railway fell on hard times in the 1940s when slate traffic dried up, but was rescued from oblivion by preservationists who were so enamoured with its quaint qualities that they acquired and restored the line. Today it serves as popular historic attraction and operates a variety of exceptional old steam locomotives in excursion service. Locomotive Talyllyn dates from 1864 making it among the oldest serviceable locomotives in Britain.

Daily excursions are run from April to October with occasional services and special events offered off-season. Talyllyn's Tywyn Wharf station is just a short walk from the British rail stop of the same name on the Cambrian Coast line, services are provided by Arriva Trains Wales. The line was the subject of the charming 1965 film, *Railway with a Heart of Gold*, that has encouraged people to visit the railway over the years. Talyllyn, Ffestiniog and Welsh Highland Railways are among the finest of the Welsh narrow-gauge lines. Also of interest are the Vale of Rheidol Railway, and Bala Lake Railway, which may be best enjoyed with a Great Little Trains of Wales rail 'Wanderer' ticket. The nearby Snowdon Mountain Railway requires a separate fare.

Below: Talyllyn's diminutive tank locomotive Sir Haydn was built in 1878 and is nearly as old as the railway itself.

SEVERN VALLEY

Bucolic Journey in the Cradle of the Industrial Revolution

Brian Solomon

The Severn – Britain's longest river – winds a 180-mile (290-km) semicircular course from headwaters in the Welsh mountains before reaching the Severn estuary from where it flows to the Celtic Sea via the Bristol Channel. It passes through regions famous as crucibles of the 18th-century industrial revolution. Coalbrookdale on the Severn was the location of an intensive early iron industry, and is the site of the famous cast-iron bridge built by John Wilkinson and Abraham Darby between 1773 and 1779.

The rise of the iron and coal industries were key to the development of the steam railway in Britain in the early 19th century. Downriver from Coalbrookdale is one of Britain's most loved lines; the Severn Valley Railway which runs for 16.5 miles (26.5 km) through an especially scenic portion of its namesake valley. Opened in 1862, for more than a century this line served as a lightly used through-route connecting Shrewsbury with Bewdley and Kidderminster, tapping coal industries and pastoral villages along the way. Its scenery was well appreciated by railway travellers, but unfortunately this didn't impress Dr Richard Beeching, the chairman of British Railways, whose infamous recommendations in the early 1960s resulted in draconian trimming of the nationalized company's network. The short-sighted severing of the Severn Valley line as a through-route occurred in 1963. To rescue the line, The Severn Valley Railway Society was formed in 1965. Limited operations as a preserved railway began in 1970, and by 1984 the line had been restored from Bridgnorth to Kidderminster – where it connects with the mainline network.

Since that time it has been developed into one of Britain's finest historic lines. In addition to tracks and trains, it features wonderfully restored passenger stations

Opposite above: A signalman works the levers at Arley signal box. Although Severn Valley Railway staff are largely volunteers, this signal box plays a vital role in train operations so staff here are qualified.

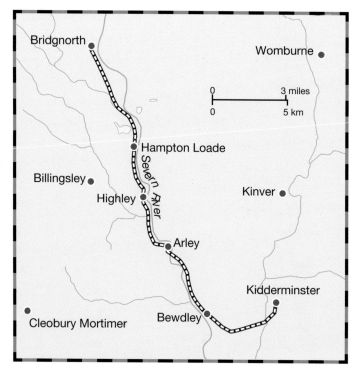

Opposite below: The Severn Valley offers more than just preserved steam locomotives: it provides the experience of a classic British branch from the pre-grouping Great Western Railway network in the 1930–1940s period. A GWR locomotive has the signal at Arley to proceed towards Bewdley.

and signal boxes, engine sheds and other period railway infrastructure that allow visitors to step back in time to when Britain's railways reigned supreme. SVR runs trains using numerous serviceable steam locomotives and more than five dozen restored carriages that span various periods.

The best way to reach the SVR is to take mainline services to Kidderminster. SVR runs a seasonal schedule of trains varying from four to seven round trips daily, with more trains available for special events. In the winter, there is a limited service with trains only operating on certain days. It is best to choose a day with a full complement of trains to allow for stop-overs at stations along the line.

On the run from Kidderminster to Bewdley trains pass through the 439 Bewdley Tunnel. Bewdley itself is an old junction station and features two working signal boxes, one at each end of the station. Just beyond the station is the magnificent stone eight-arch Wribbenhall Viaduct. The line then meanders for nearly 4 miles (6.4 km) towards Arley, crossing the cast-iron Victoria Bridge over the Severn a short distance before the station. Arley retains all the charm of a classic rural railway station and makes for a perfect mid-trip place to stop. As with many of SVR's stations, this features a passing loop and active signal box. Several pleasant walks are possible from Arley. Head down the road, perhaps stop at the local pub for a pint of bitter and 'bangers and mash', then work off lunch by following the footpath back along the Severn towards the Victoria Bridge. Arley is also home to a popular arboretum.

Beyond Arley the line continues upriver for 2.5 miles (4 km) to Highley, which is the location of another passing loop, a small yard and SVR's engine house – often open to visitors. After another 2 miles (3.2 km) the line reaches the quiet station of Hampton Loade, and then after 4 more miles (6.4 km) it comes to the end of the line at Bridgnorth. The pleasant combination of rural scenery, slow-paced vintage trains and classic villages makes for one of the world's most memorable railway experiences. While a round trip can be accomplished in as little as three hours, most visitors choose to make a day of the experience. One excursion over the line just whets the palate for another!

Opposite above: Restored British Railways 'Black Five' 45110 works upgrade toward the station at Highley on the Severn Valley Railway.

Above: A light drizzle greets a steam train as it approaches the rural halt at Hampton Loade on the run from Kidderminster to Bridgnorth. Semaphores, steam locomotives and lush scenery are among Severn Valley's many attractions.

Opposite below: In addition to its regular schedule, Severn Valley accommodates special charter trains such as this wedding special at Bewdley.

LEGENDARY LA ROBLA

The Tale of a Survivor

Fred Matthews

'The railway that refused to die' was the description given by the historian Mike Bent (in the magazine *Today's Railways* no. 139, 2007) to the most remarkable railway revival in Iberia, the sinuous 207-mile (333-km) La Robla metre-gauge line, which runs diagonally across northern Spain from the ancient cathedral city of Léon on the northern edge of the great central high plain, the Meseta, to the busy modern metropolis of Bilbao on the Bay of Biscay. The two cities embody different cultures – Léon, the Castilian world of piety, order and dignity, and Bilbao, the urban Basque world of energy, creative innovation and opportunity.

The La Robla line, which is now part of the government narrow-gauge system FEVE, has survived in part due to a major coal-fired power plant near its line – but

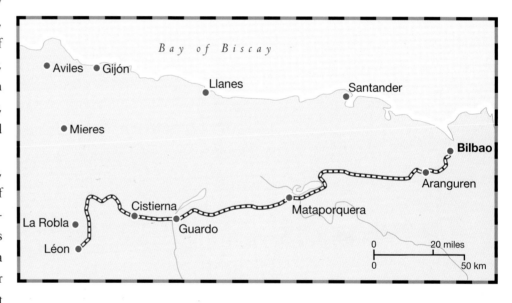

also due to the regional authorities' sense of history. La Robla, nicknamed 'El Hullero' (the Miner), opened in 1894, originally running from the mining town of the same name, and it developed slowly as a freight hauler, since Basque industry found other coal sources of higher quality. From 1917, and especially during the era of self-sufficiency under General Franco (1940–58), the line became one of the busiest of all narrow-gauge railways, with over 60 steam locos, including several Beyer-Garratts, cramming its unsignalled single track. After 1960, as the Spanish economy opened up to the world, traffic declined steadily, until the ultimate indignity came in around 2000 when the remaining power plant began receiving fuel from abroad, trans-shipped at Mataporquera.

Opposite: Belle Epoque splendour: Bilbao's Concordia Station, or Estacion de Santander, built in 1898, is the most striking survivor from the city's glory days as port and industrial centre. Behind the façade are two platforms, hosting a couple of Santander trains and the single round trip to Léon. Hourly electric locals to Balmaseda keep the pigeons awake.

Now there is still some sand traffic carried to a glassworks and container trains from Bilbao also operate on occasion. Otherwise the route is travelled by locals and tourists in equal measure.

As important as the freight traffic was the role that La Robla served for the Meseta's youth – it provided a lifeline out of the drudgery of peasant agriculture into the perilous, but more lucrative, world of urban industry and commerce. For many years the 11-hour daily *Correo* hauled Mesetans towards opportunity and occasionally back for family visits. A tradition not wholly gone – on Friday afternoons the railcar from Bilbao's art nouveau Concordia Station is replaced by a four-car historic train, including cafeteria, which returns on Sunday. In both directions, the scheduled through-train follows the old Spanish custom of a lunchtime departure (14.00 from Léon, 14.30 from Bilbao), arriving 7½ hours later.

During the first six hours out of Léon, *El Hullero*'s ever-twisting route passes interesting villages and (in season) nesting storks, while many derelict mining and loading facilities still dot the rocky hills of the line's western section. The splendid Cantabrian mountains loom to the north. It will be after dark most of the year when it pulls out of Bercedo-Montija, travelling along the hillside as the landscape drops away to reveal the Cadagua valley. The train descends steeply along the mountainside to FEVE's workshop town of Balmaseda and then on the electric suburban track to Bilbao Concordia. Perhaps the trip is best made starting from Bilbao, so that the stunning churches of Léon beckon the following morning.

THE SPANISH AVE

Across Spain by High-Speed Train

Brian Solomon

High-speed rail is the sexiest modern railway technology. Countries that have pioneered high-speed rail technology take great national pride in pushing the speed envelope. Japan's *Shinkansen* is the most famous, followed by the French *Train à Grande Vitesse* (*TGV*). By contrast, some countries have been content to import and adapt high-speed technology to suit their own needs. Spain has done a little of both. It developed and promoted advanced train technology in the form of the TALGO system, and it has imported high-speed trains from France and Germany. TALGO was originally conceived as a lightweight train with a low centre of gravity, and the system has been further refined as a tilting train (to allow greater speeds through curves by reducing the effects of centrifugal forces on passengers), and more recently adapted with gauge-changing technology.

In the 1990s Spain imported the French high-speed system. It built new high-speed lines to connect its most important cities and these initially hosted specially

Opposite: A Spanish-built TALGO pendular train works an AVE intercity service on the high-speed line at Almodovar del Rio, Spain. Using a passive tilting system, the TALGO pendular can be operated fast through curves without passengers feeling the ill-effects of centrifugal forces. Also this is the gauge-changing TALGO that provides through-services over standard-gauge and broad-gauge routes.

styled *TGV*-like trains – marketed as *Alta Velocidad Española* (*AVE*) – and gauge-changing TALGO's marketed under several names including *Avant* and *Avala*.

While most of the Spanish railway network uses the Iberian broad gauge (5 feet 6 inches/1,676 mm between rail heads), most European networks have used the Stephenson standard gauge established in Britain in the 1820s (4 feet 8½ inches/1,435 mm between railheads), so Spain's newly built high-speed lines use the more common gauge. The first *AVE* route opened in 1992, connecting Madrid, Córdoba and Seville. Very fast *AVE* services ply this route at half-hourly intervals. With a top speed of 186 mph (300 km/h), most *AVE* trains are scheduled to cover the 292 miles (470 km) in just 2 hours 30 minutes. The ride is smooth as silk as Spanish track is some of the finest in the world. The train's schedule is guaranteed too. If an *AVE* train runs more than five minutes late, passengers are refunded. But timekeeping is so good that very few refunds are issued. These are some of Europe's most luxurious trains, where movies can be enjoyed onboard as the Spanish plains flash by.

Above: An Alta Velocidad Española *glides along near Almodovar del Rio, Spain at 186 mph (300 km/h) – the top speed on the line.*

The success of Spain's first high-speed route has led to ambitious network plans. The Madrid–Valladolid *AVE* route and an extension to Malaga opened in 2007, Madrid–Barcelona in 2008 and Madrid–Valencia in 2011. Other high-speed extensions include a branch of the Madrid-Barcelona route to Huesca; and a branch of the Madrid-Valencia route to Albacete. In mid-2013, a long-planned connection to the French high-speed TGV system was opened to lead to TGV through services between Barcelona and Paris. Ultimately, it may be possible to take a through high-speed train over the combined AVE-TGV system from Paris all the way to Seville or Malaga.

Among the most modern Spanish high-speed trains sets are TALGO-Bombardier built examples colloquially known as *Pato* (duck) because of the pronounced duck-bill-styled front end. In addition to these 186-mph (300-km/h) trains, TALGO gauge-changing trains that travel at more moderate speeds allow fast through-services to take advantage of the Iberian-gauge network.

Opposite: Spanish AVE *trains at the modern AVE terminal in Seville. Spain's first AVE high-speed train sets were distinctively styled adaptations of the French TGV trains.*

OVER THE TATRAS

From Prague to the Ukrainian Frontier

Brian Solomon

Czechoslovakia was carved out of remnants of the Austro-Hungarian Empire after the end of the First World War. Much of the railway network had been built to fulfil the needs of the old empire, mainline routes tended to connect and radiate from important imperial centres: Vienna, Budapest, Olomouc and Prague. Complicating the history, Czech areas of Bohemia, Moravia and portions of Silesia had been situated in the Austrian parts of the empire, while Slovakia was largely in Hungarian parts. As a result, at the time of Czechoslovak union there were inadequate railway connections between these historic regions. During the Czech-Slovak union railway lines between these regions were developed and improved.

Czechoslovakia's relatively short existence was fraught with political turmoil as a result of the German invasion and occupation during the Second World War, and the exercise of Communist control after the war. Democracy was restored between 1989 and 1992, and in 1993 the nations agreed to a divide along ethnic

Opposite: A České Dráhy (CD) locomotive leads a westward Slovak Republic Railways (ŽSR) InterCity train at Štrba, Slovakia – the summit of the Tatra route. The splendid Slovakian scenery is the highlight of the run from Košice to Prague.

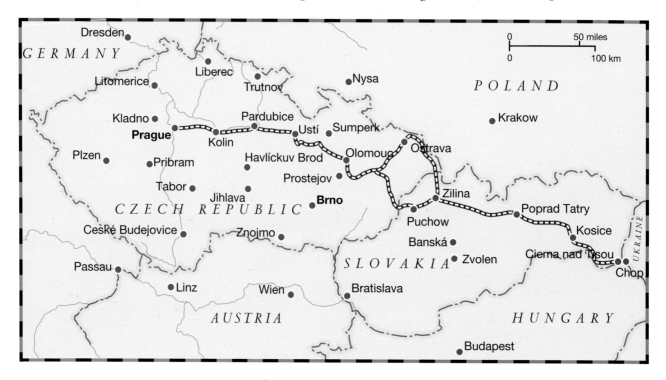

lines, becoming the Czech Republic in the west and Slovak Republic in the east. As a result of the split, the former Československé Státné Dráhy (Czechoslovak State Railways) was similarly divided, with the new České Dráhy (CD) and Žekeznice Slovenjskej Republiky (Slovak Republic Railways or ŽSR) serving their respective countries. Later, to comply with European Union directives, the railways were further sub-divided into distinct infrastructure and operating companies.

Although the railways are now separate, the long union between these networks, and the desire to operate through-services, has resulted in an unusually high level of cooperation between railways in the region. Today, through-trains running between Prague (Praha) and points in Slovakia routinely mix equipment from both countries, and locomotives and cars cross borders daily. Furthermore, since much of the locomotive fleet dates to before the split, equipment types are common to both countries, the only differences now being in their paint livery and lettering.

Both Czech and Slovak Railways operate complex networks with numerous main routes and branches. In general, services on main lines are very good and trains operate at regular intervals throughout the day. Among the most interesting and pleasant long-distance trips is the one running east from Prague across the Czech Republic into Slovakia and over the Tatras to the eastern Slovak city of

Above: Freights ascending the Tatras require assistance from 'banking' locomotives that work at the back of the train. This train carries heavy steel plate from the US Steel Works in Košice. An antique, but immaculately maintained, six-motor electric shoves at the back.

Košice. Many long-distance trains on this route depart from Prague's main railway station (Praha Hlavni Nádraži), an elegant art nouveau masterpiece characterized by the carved stone snakes and faces displayed on its exterior façade. Inside, the main waiting room could be mistaken for the atrium of a concert hall or luxurious early 20th-century hotel. Tracks are served under a sizeable twin-span steel and glass train shed, which has been renovated in recent years with modern platforms. A few trains also depart from Prague's international station, located to the north of the city centre, but it lacks comparable charm and style.

Different grades of service work the mainline to the east. The fastest, most modern and most expensive services use imported Pendolino tilting trains. These depart at two-hour intervals for Olomouc and Ostrava, with a few Pendolino runs continuing on to Bohumin. A more traditional experience is offered by InterCity and EuroCity trains that operate using conventional locomotive-hauled consists. Some of these only operate to border towns, but a few, including overnight sleeping car trains, provide through-services to Košice and beyond to the Ukraine.

Among the nicest and most interesting runs is EC121 the *Košičan* which departs Nádraži Praha Hlavni mid-morning and runs via the Tatras mountains through to Košice, arriving there in early evening. Like most EC runs, first-class

Below: Line relocations, such as this one near Lupěné, Czech Republic, have shortened the run between Prague and eastern Czech cities. Here a new tunnel allows for a direct route through the hillside; vestiges of the old route are seen to the left. Tilting Pendolino trains also allow for faster running.

carriages are available, and they are generally worth the extra money as they tend to be more comfortable and less crowded at peak times.

The entire route is electrified and the condition of the infrastructure is excellent. The heavily travelled route east of Prague hosts a variety of local and express passenger trains as well as numerous freight trains. Initially much of the terrain east of Prague is characterized by rolling agricultural fields with some industry. At Kolin is found an important junction with a line that hosts freight traffic from the northern Czech Republic and Germany. Beyond Česká Třebova is another important junction, where the line to Brno, Břeclav and Vienna diverges. To the east the line winds through rugged scenery, but avoids the more mountainous terrain to the south.

In recent years, some line relocations have straightened the route, using tunnels to avoid circuitous sections that previously wound through river valleys. Olomouc is a big station. While the station may look dreary compared with Prague, don't be deceived: Olomouc is well worth a stopover. At one time it was capital of Moravia, and resembles a smaller version of Prague with fascinating intricate architecture and beautiful central squares. The city centre is easily reached by a tram ride south from the station. Tram tickets can be purchased from vending machines outside the station.

Beyond Olomouc, the main route uses an avoiding line around the busy railway junction at Přerov. At Hranice na Moravě the lines east divide: many long-distance trains take the northerly route that loops through the heavily industrialized cities of Ostrava, Bohumin and Český Těšin; however the *Košičan* runs along the more scenic southerly route via Vsetin and across the border to Púchov and then north to Žilina, Slovakia. Here the two routes come back together.

The ride east from Žilina is the highlight of the trip. Leaving Žilina the line hugs the River Váh for many miles. (At Vrútky, there are connections to a diesel-service that runs southward through rugged mountain scenery featuring looping curves and tunnels to Banská Bystrica and beyond to Zvolen.) In places the river, railway and highway cluster tightly together through narrow passes. An enormous dam west of Bešeňová (built between 1969 and 1975) holds back a large man-made lake that flooded 13 villages. The railway loops through a pair of sweeping horseshoe curves to gain elevation around the lake, resulting in some interesting views of the line, especially if you are fortunate enough to pass another train in the middle of the curves.

Above: A CD electric catches the sun in front of Prague's main railway station (Nádraži Praha Hlavni). This station features a twin-span steel and glass train shed and elegant art nouveau head house.

After crossing the River Belá at Liptovský, the line climbs away from the Váh on its ascent of the Tatras. The summit is reached at the saddle in the mountains at Štrba, 2,789 feet (850 m) above sea level. Here connections are available to the 3-mile (4.75-km) long, steeply graded rack line operated as the Štrbske Pleso-Štrba Railway, which connects with a network of narrow-gauge tram lines that serve Tatra mountain resorts. The mainline descends the Tatra grade to Poprad Tatry, an industrialized town that also features connections to the narrow-gauge Tatra-tram network. Beyond the line runs via the scenic Hornád River valley to Košice. Here the old town offers classic central European charm. Connections are available south to Hungary, and east into the Ukraine. At the Ukrainian border a gauge change is required for through-cars since Ukrainian railways use the Russian 5 foot (1,524 mm) gauge. Although a broad-gauge line serves the Košice steel mill complex, there are no regular passenger services on this line, and passenger trains use the parallel 4 feet 8½ inch (1,435 mm) line to the Ukrainian frontier.

From the Bohemian capital to the summit of the Tatras and beyond, this journey offers a window on places rarely visited during the Cold War years, and yet it remains a mainline railway interlude often missed by intrepid travellers.

Below: A CD class 162 electric whisks an InterCity train westward through Lipník, Czech Republic. Czech railway infrastructure is among the best in Eastern Europe and is heavily utilized by a mix of freight and passenger trains.

RUSSIA'S SECRET RAILWAY

The BAM Route across Siberia

Colin Nash

The Baikal Amur Mainline (BAM) is a $59\,^5/_6$-inch (1,520-mm) gauge railway, 2,687 miles (4,324 km) long. It runs parallel with and to the north of the Trans-Siberian Railway in the former Soviet Union and was built as a strategic alternative to that railway which was considered vulnerable, particularly along Russia's sensitive border with China. Much of the line was built over permafrost which necessitated the use of special durable tracks in its construction. The line runs from Tayshet in the west to the coastal town of Sovetskaya Gavan on the Straits of Tartary in the east, and for much of the route it is single track.

The BAM has a colourful, if slightly sinister, history. Work started in the 1930s, using slave labour from Stalin's gulag camps and many labourers lost their lives during its construction. In the Far Eastern section, built during the Second World War, work was carried out by prisoners of war and it is estimated that as many as 150,000 died building the line. After Stalin's death in 1953 all work stopped and was not recommenced until 1974. The line was not finally completed until 1991, but it was largely underused both due to its military sensitivity, which meant that visitors to the region were not encouraged, and the collapse of the Soviet Union, which resulted in the cancellation of many mining projects along the route. Towns that were originally built for the construction workers were also not viable after its completion.

However, lately there have been moves to reinvigorate the BAM. The improving economic situation in Russia has meant that there is renewed mining activity and plans to increase container traffic using the route. A 9½-mile (15.34-km) long tunnel at Severomuyski has taken some 25 miles (40 km) off the route removing the need for banking engines over the heavy gradients and there are tentative plans to recommence the building of a tunnel at the eastern end of the line, originally begun under Stalin, to link Sakhalin Island to the mainland.

Opposite: At Kuanda station, the Golden Link Monument symbolizes the uniting of two sections of the BAM in 1985.

Above: *The Bureya River Bridge, a 1,200-yard (1.1-km) steel truss bridge carrying the BAM eastwards from Tynda. It is one of 11 major river bridges on the route.*

The BAM is being increasingly used by Western tourists as a great way to explore the secret parts of Russia. Railway enthusiasts, too, are taking the opportunity to see how the railway operates in one of the more obscure areas of this vast country. There is a daily train from Tynda to Komsomolsk with a journey time of 38 hours but it is more usual to make a trip on this railway part of a seven-day package which allows travellers time to stop off and experience the sights and culture of Siberia.

Typical of the traction on the BAM are diesel locomotives of the TE10 series with two- and three-unit variants of the TE10V, TE10M and TE10U models all being represented together with four-unit TE10C engines for use in the difficult northern winter conditions. Electric traction is currently typically provided by VL65 and VL80K locomotives together with E5K and EP1J. Passengers are accommodated in private compartments with seats that convert into sleeping berths. Although some food is usually provided, prices are very inflated so it is normal for travellers to bring their own and share. A samovar of hot water is also usually provided in each car to enable passengers to make hot drinks and soups but alcohol is not allowed on trains in Russia and its consumption could result in the miscreant being put off the train in the middle of nowhere by the Provodnitsa who is invariably a woman and responsible, amongst other things, for issuing sheets for the sleeping berths – which have to be rented at extra cost.

A journey on the BAM gives the traveller the unforgettable experience of passing through the vast wastes of Siberia with its swamps, lakes and rivers and with most of the landscape sealed in permafrost. Upon leaving Tayshet trains head westwards crossing over the top of Bratsk dam to reach Ust-Kut – the end of the line until 1974. After crossing the Kirenga River trains skirt the northern shore of Lake Baikal and head northeast up the valley of the Upper Angara River, through Severomuyski Tunnel – newly opened in 2003 and 27 years in construction – into one of the most scenic sections of the route towered over by mountains to the north and south. At Taksimo the electrified section of the line ends and trains are diesel-hauled for the rest of the journey. After crossing numerous rivers, trains reach Kuanda where the official opening of the line took place in 1984.

Beyond Kuanda the line crosses the Kodar Mountains, known as the Siberian Alps, to reach Khami, its most northerly point before running along the Olyokma River to Tynda. Continuing eastwards the BAM runs along the north shore of the Zeya Reservoir before crossing it over the 1,200-yard (1.1-km) long Bureya River Bridge. The line then passes through the 1¼-mile (2-km) long Dussi-Alin Tunnel under the Bureinsky range and enters the Amgun River valley. To the east lies Evoron Lake, home to many species of wild geese, heron, hawks, eagles and

Above left: Train no. 76 at Severobaikalsk station bound for Tynda.

curlew before trains head southeast to cover the 87-mile (140-km) section to Komsomolsk, where the daily service from Tayshet terminates: a journey of 915 miles (1,473 km).

Most visitors leave the train at Komsomolsk and head for Khabarovsk in order to take the Trans-Siberian to Vladivostok. The BAM line itself continues to Sovetskaya Gavan. There is one train a day, two in summer, and the journey takes 15 hours. This section was completed in 1945 and was the first section of the BAM to be opened. The area becomes increasingly more militarized as it approaches the sea as it services the air and naval bases there.

After crossing the Amur River trains head down the Selikhin branch and enter the UNESCO World Heritage Region of the Sikhote Alin Mountains. The region plays host to the widest variety of animals in the world ranging from brown bears and reindeer to tropical species, such as leopards, tigers and the Asiatic black bear. Beyond the mountains lies the Russian air base of Mongokhto, at one time the largest in the Soviet Far East. The line travels on to Vanino, an important port on the Straits of Tartary and the mainland terminal for the train ferry to Sakhalin Island. From Vanino the train ferry takes trains to the port of Kholmsk on Sakhalin Island. Kholmsk is effectively the end of passenger services as Sovetskaya Gavan itself is a naval base.

Above: *Having just passed through the Severobaikalsk tunnel, train no 76 now skirts the snow-capped Severomuisk Range.*

A journey along the BAM offers a unique opportunity to see a part of the world well away from the usual tourist haunts. It is not numbered among the most popular destinations but is recommended for those seeking a more adventurous experience. That experience includes the wild desolate beauty of Siberia and the people and creatures that live there. This is a never-to-be-forgotten adventure set amongst mountains and lakes in the vastness of one of the world's great wilderness landscapes.

TO THE LAND OF THE MIDNIGHT SUN

North of the Arctic Circle to Narvik, Norway

Brian Solomon

One of the world's most northerly railways is the iron-ore-hauling line that extends through the top of Sweden, beyond the Arctic circle, to Norway's ice-free port at Narvik. This is sometimes called the Lapland Railway in English, while in Swedish it is known as Mainbanan, and the last few miles in Norway are known in Norwegian as the Ofotbanen. This railway connects with the rest of the Swedish network south of the Arctic circle at Boden (with a secondary connection at Gallivare). The southern end of the line from Boden to Luleå was part of the original construction and remains important for the trans-shipment of iron ore to sea-vessels at Svartön Harbour on the Gulf of Bothnia at the northern reaches of the Baltic Sea.

Built to tap rich iron reserves in northern Sweden, the first section from Luleå to Gällivare (44 miles/70 km north of the Arctic circle) was opened in 1888. It reached Kiruna in 1899, while the final portion running across the border with Norway to Narvik was finished during 1902–3. In its first decades, steam locomotives worked trains, but the volume of heavy ore trains made it an early candidate for overhead electrification; this was completed on the line between 1915 and the mid-1920s.

Today, the line remains a primary ore conduit, and hosts some of the heaviest freight trains in Europe with typically loaded ore trains weighing in the vicinity of 8,500 tons (8,620 tonnes). While these are not nearly as heavy as freights in North America where coal trains routinely run at 13,500-16,000 tons (13,700-16,300 tonnes), they are two to three times heavier than most big freights in

Opposite: On a long summer evening a short local passenger train led by an RC electric departs Gällivare, Sweden for Narvik, Norway. The junction with the ore-hauling branch to Malmbenget and Svappavaara can be seen to the left just beyond the train.

continental Europe and require some of the world's most powerful electrics to haul them. Ore is produced at mines at Malmbenget near Gällivare, off a branch to Svappavaara, and at Kiruna. When mines are working at capacity, ten to 14 loaded trains daily work northwards to Narvik, with half as many working south to Luleå. In addition, container trains serve the port of Narvik, and three daily passenger trains work the northern end of the line. Most of the railway is built with single track with dual passing sidings constructed at regular intervals to allow trains to pass and overtake one another. The railway is fluid and most trains are tightly scheduled.

A through overnight sleeping car train runs daily from Stockholm to Narvik. This departs northbound from Stockholm Central in the early evening for a 13-hour run overnight to Boden, where connections are available to Luleå. It continues the remaining 271 miles (437 km) to Narvik, with the most spectacular parts of the journey coming in the last 100 miles (160 km). Crossing the Arctic circle is anticlimactic; this seemingly important geographical divide is featureless geographically. Gällivare is 104 miles (168 km) beyond Boden and is the first major station in the Arctic where the midnight sun reigns from 2 June to 12 July. A classic wooden building on the east side of the line serves both

passengers and as an operations centre. North of the station is a small yard and junction, where the secondary line running south to Östersund terminates.

Kiruna is Sweden's northernmost city and supports a population of more than 18,000 people. It has an interesting railway station and sizeable locomotive shops, but the town itself is largely composed of nondescript modern buildings. Historically it was integrally tied to the mining of iron ore. However, since the 1990s Kiruna has looked to attract tourists to the surrounding natural splendour, and appealing to winter adventurers by offering dog-sledding trips. Recently, on-going iron ore operations have undermined portions of Kiruna forcing significant relocation of the city. In 2012, a new diversion line was opened bypassing the town to the east. As of 2013, the old station was still served on stub-end of the

Opposite above: Far north of the Arctic circle an RC-6 electric leads the northward overnight train from Stockholm along Sweden's Torneträsk. In mid-summer the sun stays above the horizon for more than a month.

Above: A local passenger train lays over at Kiruna, Sweden. In August 2012, this became a stub-end station when a new diversionary line opened to bypass portions of the city undermined by mining activities.

Opposite below: A southward local passenger train exits the snow sheds at Rikgränsen, Sweden. This is the highest point on the line and is located on the border between Sweden and Norway.

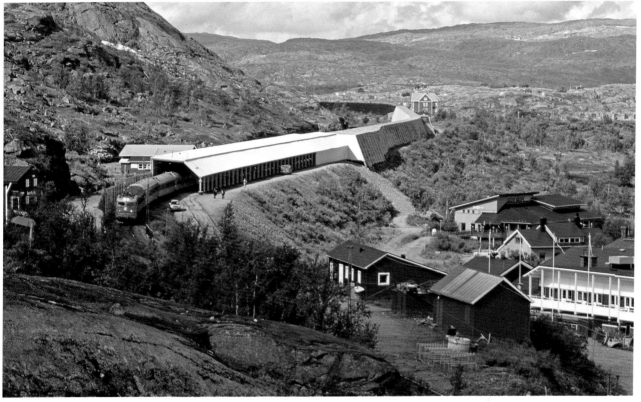

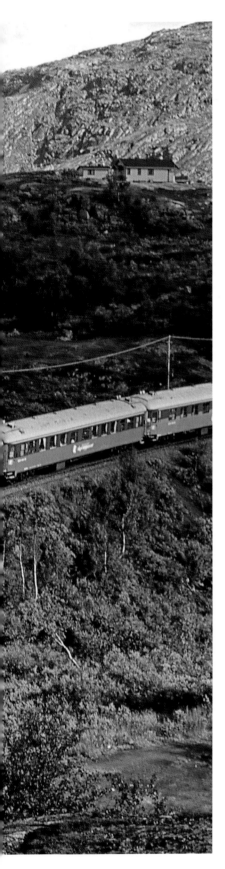

old mainline, but this is expected to close eventually. The best of the scenery appears after Kiruna and much of it is better appreciated from the right-hand side of the train.

North of Kiruna the line turns in a westerly direction. Its runs for many miles on a shelf above the serene Arctic lake called Torneträsk. A remote station of this name is located near the east end of the lake. Here is one of many large, but disused, brick substations that date from the original electrification. The Arctic tundra stretches away for miles beyond the lake. In mid-summer the sun never sets here, which can be disorienting to those who have never experienced 24-hour daylight before. Instead of dipping below the horizon, the sun travels north, which can confuse your natural sense of direction as well as your sleep habits.

Visitors to Sweden's Abisko National Park – established in 1909 – use the Abisko Turiststation. Further north the line navigates a 1,200-yard (1,100-m) tunnel beneath Mt Njula. The railway crests its highest point at Rikgränsen on the border between Sweden and Norway. This is the location of the world's northernmost ski-resort. The station is partially covered by a snow shed. Across the border to Norway, at Bjørnfell the line navigates a series of twisting curves, passing through numerous snow sheds and snow fences designed to keep drifts off the line. The final leg of the journey offers stunning views of the Ofotjorden (Ofot Fjord), as the line descends rapidly towards Narvik.

Narvik has flourished primarily because of its role in exporting iron ore. In April 1940 it was famously seized by the German army to secure the flow of Swedish ore for the German war machine. Fierce sea battles raged in the fjord, and fighting continued along the railway line, with a battle being fought near Bjørnfell. Today, it marks the end of the line. This portion of the Norwegian railway is only connected via the Swedish link, and is thus isolated from the rest of Norway's network.

The wild, open and unspoiled landscape north of the Artic circle presents a rail adventure that only gets more exciting as the train makes its way further north. Yet, as it reaches the port of Narvik, passengers may conclude that the most spectacular views were across the Torneträsk, which offers a rare glimpse into the wilderness, the land beyond being so remote few people will ever experience it first-hand.

Left: *The Narvik–Stockholm overnight train catches a ray of sun between snow sheds at Bjørnfjell, Norway. It takes the train more than 21 hours to make the full run.*

TUSCAN TREASURES

Two Hidden Rural Routes

Fred Matthews

Tuscany is one of the most thoroughly explored and appreciated areas in the world and yet two small railways tucked away in its mountainous northwest have remained relatively unknown to foreigners. They provide the perfect way of discovering the delights of the countryside at leisure. They differ greatly in history and original purpose but share a special fascination.

The Porrettana Railway, which now runs as two connected branch lines through the Apennines between Bologna and Pistoia, was for 70 years (until 1934) a busy, important and difficult part of the original main line between Lombardy and central Italy. From Bologna (elevation 165 feet/50 m) the line rises gradually up the Reno valley to Porretta Terme and the summit at Pracchia (2030 feet/619 m), then plunges 1,817 feet in 15 miles (554 m in 24 km) to Pistoia. The line is tortuous, with a tunnel 1½ miles (2.4 km) long south of Pracchia, the summit, followed by a high viaduct over the Ombrone River. Thick forest cover restricts views but at Corbezzi the treeline breaks to allow a wonderful view of the valley and Monte Albano beyond.

The Porrettana was electrified in 1927, ending what must have been one of the great dramas of the steam age. Then, in the early 1930s, after many years of construction, the new Bologna–Florence Direttissima was opened, cutting the express time between the cities from 4¼ to 1¼ hours (it's now 40 minutes with a new super direct line, almost all underground). The Bologna–Porretta line hosts hourly railcars and there is also an irregular service between Pistoia and Porretta.

The second rail treasure has always been obscure. It was built at the end of the 19th century to open the Garfagnana, the scenic, historic and impoverished valley between the Apuan Alps and the Apennines in the far northwest of Tuscany. The route traverses 56 twisting miles (90 km) north from the medieval city of Lucca up through the increasingly narrow Serchio valley, then passes through

two long tunnels as it turns west into the rockier, even-more isolated Lunigiana, terminating at castle-dominated Aulla, on the secondary line from Parma to La Spezia. Architectural and scenic sites dot both the Garfagnana and the Lunigiana – the Garfagnana hosts several Romanesque churches as well as the striking, stone Devil's Bridge, built in the 11th century after (legend says) the Devil was bribed with the soul of the first creature crossing it. A dog was sent first. In the wild Lunigiana are two notable, isolated villages, Equi Terme (with an ancient cave containing fossil dogs) and picturesque Monzone, perched on a hillside like a tiny Mont St Michel.

This remarkable route has sparse service, especially in the Lunigiana, which allows occasional steam train excursions, but it's worth considering a one-way trip, continuing from Aulla to either Parma or La Spezia, both tourist centres.

Above: Porrettana: a 1980s-style electric railcar set unloads its corporal's guard of passengers at Porretta Terme, having come up the mountainside from Pistoia and then dropped from the summit at Pracchia. Through-passengers for Bologna will have a few minutes' wait until the similar railcar from Bologna arrives and reverses direction.

HUNDRED VALLEYS

The Stunning Centovalli

Fred Matthews

The best way to approach the striking international electric railway nicknamed the 'Centovalli' (hundred valleys) is the way the residents of the Suisse Romande (the French-speaking western part of Switzerland) do. Arriving from Geneva or Lausanne, the passengers detrain in the Italian town of Domodossola and move towards the locomotive where there is a sign indicating 'Locarno' with a large arrow pointing straight down.

This is the beginning of a remarkably varied, metre-gauge electric line that runs the 31 miles (50 km) from the short tunnel in Domodossola to a longer tunnel ending beneath the Swiss Federal station in Locarno, the sunny resort on Lake Maggiore. During the intervening hundred minutes, the little trains with their big picture windows traverse a landscape of steep hills, forests, valleys and chasms, high viaducts and picturesque villages dominated by tall-steepled churches. Leaving Domodossola, the train briefly reaches its maximum speed of about 38 mph (61 km/h) across a valley, before tackling a classic continental zigzag on 6 per cent grades up the hillside, passing an apparently deserted medieval village, to reach the once-isolated Val Vigezzo, 1,000 feet and more (over 300 m) above Domodossola. At first the train runs along the southerly hillside above the Melezza River and its tiny spa towns, then it descends to curve through verdant meadows approaching the Swiss border at Camedo, 20 miles (32 km) from the starting point.

Opposite: The Centovalli Railway route celebrated its 90th year of through-rail operation in 2013. The line is jointly run by the Swiss Ferrovie Autolinee Regionali Ticinesi and Italian Società Subalpina di Imprese Ferroviarie.

Entering Switzerland, the train commences the truly stunning 'centovalli' section, clinging to a narrow cliff above the deep Melezza gorge, crossing endless side-streams, with the river sometimes visible far below. The next 6 miles (10 km) boast hourly local trains along with eight to 11 international expresses. There is a reason for the hourly all-stops locals. The population of the surrounding area is small and scattered; but we are now in super-efficient Switzerland, with signed footpaths from each halt and two aerial cableways from Verdasio, one of them up across the valley to the single-street stone village of Rasa, reachable otherwise by footpath.

Around a right-angled bend into a broader section of the Melezza valley, the train arrives at Intragna, a picturesque vertical village, with two gourmet restaurants, a Baroque church with lofty steeple and another cableway to the hills. The 230-foot (70-m) belltower dating from 1775 looks out over the Isorno canyon to the north, bridged by an Eiffel-esque, 250-foot (76-m) high iron viaduct, where bungee-jumpers can often be seen seeking their thrills. For the remaining 6 miles (10 km) the route traverses a more settled area with neat villages, then enters the 1-mile (1.6-km) long tunnel running under traffic-choked Locarno.

This remarkable railway has had a troubled life. Built to open up a scenic, but impoverished, area, it was organized in 1907 but finished only in 1923, with Swiss financial bailouts to the Italian SSIF (Società Subalpina di Imprese Ferroviarie), which shares operation with the Swiss FART (Ferrovie Autolinee Regionali Ticinese). In the 1970s much of the Italian line was washed away, and it took two years to rebuild it. The survival is remarkable especially since Canton Ticino had closed most of its local railways earlier that decade. A hint why it has survived lies in the first-class compartments of Centovalli trains, which are larger than those of most Swiss local trains. This is an important connection in terms of Swiss mobility and sense of national unity.

THE BLUE TRAIN

Linking the Veldt to the Sea

Colin Nash

Born out of the dream of a pan-African railway linking the Cape to Cairo, *The Blue Train* is the ultimate in luxury train travel. In fact, the Cape to Cairo railway line only got as far as the Zambezi River but the discovery of gold and diamonds in the region led to a great upsurge of traffic and, for some, the making of a fortune. This newfound wealth spurred the development of luxury rail travel across the continent. The first of these trains were *The Union Limited* and *The Union Express*. They transported passengers from Cape Town to the gold fields in steam-hauled luxury in the 1920s. The trains boasted hot and cold running water and card tables. Their rich royal blue and cream livery soon led to the nickname, *The Blue Train*.

With the outbreak of the Second World War the service was suspended, an indication of the austerity of those times, but it was re-established in 1946. *The Blue Train* was formally adopted as the name of the train and following extensive refurbishment and updating, the service was relaunched in 1997. It has gone on to redefine the standard for luxury train travel. It is promoted as 'a magnificent moving five star hotel' – a train fit for kings and presidents.

Currently *The Blue Train* service is operated by Luxrail, which is part of South Africa's national railway operator Transnet Freight Rail, using two train sets differentiated only by the number of suites and the option of a conference car that can be used as an observation car. Onboard facilities include Butler Service, fully carpeted suites and bathrooms with marble tiles and gold fittings. Some of the bathrooms come complete with full-size bath tubs. By utilizing the two trains so that one set runs north and the other south, the operators are able to run a daily departure from each end of the route. Traction is by a fleet of diesel and electric locomotives with a top speed of 58 mph (92 km/h). This may sound slow

Opposite above: The Blue Train *threads its way through the Hex River valley past one of the many vineyards in this area of the western cape.*

Opposite below: A trio of Class 6E Bo-Bo electric locos climb their way through mountainous country at the head of The Blue Train.

but *The Blue Train*'s operators boast that the train glides through the countryside with a noise level of only 55 decibels. At this level, noise 'somewhere between the sound of soft rainfall and normal conversation is never exceeded'.

The scheduled route runs between Pretoria and Cape Town; a journey of 994 miles (1,600 km) taking 27 hours, and including an off-train excursion on the southbound journey at Kimberley, and northbound at Matjiesfontein, to take in some of the local history. Kimberley, with its links to the diamond-mining past, and Matjiesfontein, with its Victorian buildings and London lamp posts, together create the effect of a time-warp back to an earlier colonial era. The journey takes in some of the most diverse and spectacular scenery in the African subcontinent including the splendour of the Karoo with its rich flora and fauna. Here warm, sunny days are separated from the cold, inky nights by a twilight interval of black hills and purple sunsets. This is a treeless and stunted landscape – a paradise for the aardvark, rock daisy, cape raven and pied crow to name just a few of the wild animals and flowers that may be seen. And all this flashes by the window in a kaleidoscope of ever-changing views. In the days of steam, trains had to be hauled across the Karoo by locomotives with special condensing tenders to extend their range without the need to take in water in this arid terrain. Prior to their introduction, water had to be taken into the desert in special water trains.

The Blue Train can also be chartered to any destination in South Africa where the 3 feet 6 inches (1,067 mm) gauge tracks are compatible. Popular charter routes include Pretoria to Durban, Pretoria to Bakubung Game Lodge, where passengers can experience African wildlife in its natural environment over a two-night stay, and the scenic Garden Route from Cape Town to Port Elizabeth.

Above: With Table Mountain and Cape Town as the backdrop, The Blue Train *skirts the Atlantic Ocean.*

Left: Lavish table set for two in The Blue Train's *dining car.*

Opposite: The Blue Train, *hauled by three Class 5 E-1 electric locomotives, between De Doorns and Worcester and bound for Cape Town.*

DARJEELING HIMALAYAN RAILWAY

The World's Most Famous Hill Railway

Colin Nash

This Victorian masterpiece was opened in July 1881 to join the towns of Siliguri and Darjeeling in West Bengal. Darjeeling was one of several British hill stations that were widely used by government officials and their families in the days of the Raj to escape the torrid heat of the plains in summer. The line was further extended to the south in 1964 to join up with the broad-gauge railway in Assam, and where the two met the town of New Jalpaiguri was created. On India's independence in 1948 the DHR became part of Indian Railways and in 1958 part of the Northeast Frontier Zone. The line was under continuous threat of closure for many years due to the high cost of maintenance, particularly during the monsoon season, and Indian Railways wished to be rid of it. This threat was finally lifted in 1999 when it became a UNESCO World Heritage Site, one of only two railways in the world to receive this honour, and the DHR's future was assured.

These days the line is worked by a mixture of steam and diesel with one train a day diesel-hauled in each direction between New Jalpaiguri and Darjeeling and one steam-hauled between Kurseong and Darjeeling. Several tourist trains are also steam-worked between Darjeeling and Ghum. It is a 2-foot (610-mm) gauge railway which is 55 miles (88 km) long and the journey from New Jalpaiguri to Darjeeling takes some seven hours. Diesel traction on the line is provided by two NDM6 Class locomotives supplied new in 2000, but the real attraction for most people is the fleet of vintage B Class 0-4-0ST steam engines. These were designed in Britain in the 1880s and the first batch, built by Sharp Stewart in Glasgow, was delivered in 1889.

Opposite: One of the famous B Class steam engines passes close to a fruit and vegetable shop on the approach to Darjeeling.

The line closely follows the Hill Cart Road of 1869 often running immediately alongside it. This was the road that linked Siliguri with Darjeeling before the railway was built. Its closeness has necessitated the provision of more than 170 level crossings along the shared route and means that, in built-up areas along the line, the route resembles an urban tramway which requires the use of very loud horns on the train to warn people of its approach. Above Kurseong station the line runs through the bazaar and is so close to the shops and stalls as to be almost part of them. At the dramatically named Agony Point the overhang of the carriages gives the impression that the train is riding on air and in the early years passengers were advised not to leave their seats in an attempt to get a better view of the spectacular scenery in case the train plunged into the valley. The line also features the highest station in India at Ghum, where the station house and yard contain a museum. At certain times of the year it is possible to see the snow-capped peaks of the first and third highest mountains in the world: Everest and Kangchenjunga – one of the most amazing railway sights in the world.

The major features of the route, apart from the sheer magnificence of the views, are a unique series of reverses and loops with the sharpest curve having a radius of only 29 feet (8.8 m). These enable the line to climb from 328 feet (100 m) above sea level at Siliguri to 7,218 feet (2,200 m) at Darjeeling without tunnels. Originally there were five loops and six reverses but flood damage in 1942 and 1991 led to the removal of two loops. The line wages a constant battle with flooding caused by the torrential monsoon rains, and it is a tribute to the devoted railway staff that the line is re-opened with minimum delay after the rains have passed.

The Darjeeling Himalayan Railway has changed very little over the years and the quirkiness of its nature and operation has led to its rolling stock being affectionately dubbed 'Toy Trains'. Its charm has resulted in it being the location for several Bollywood films in recent years. For railway enthusiasts and tourists alike, it is an experience not to be missed.

Left: The magnificence of the scenery is just one of the reasons that the Darjeeling Himalayan Railway was designated as a UNESCO World Heritage Site in 1999.

Opposite above: *The train arrives at the former British summer resort of Darjeeling. It offers relief from India's baking summer heat that is just as welcome today as it was in the days of the Raj.*

Left: *The train crosses the line at one of the loops that allow it to climb up to 7,218 feet (2,200 m) during its journey to Darjeeling.*

Opposite below: *A diesel-hauled train threads its way through the crowded streets of Kurseong.*

JAPANESE SHINKANSEN

Route of the Bullet Train

Brian Solomon

The first Japanese *Shinkansen* ('New main line') was the world's first purpose-built super high-speed railway. Built to serve one of the most heavily populated and most industrialized areas of the world, this new separate railway, free from grade crossings and other direct interference, allowed Japanese National Railways (JNR) to augment services on its very busy Tokaido route between Tokyo and Osaka.

Where the traditional Japanese railway system uses narrow-gauge standards – its tracks are 3 feet 6 inches (1,067 mm) between the rails – the high-speed Shinkansen features the 4 feet 8½ inch (1,435 mm) standard gauge (common to most railways in Europe and North America). This broader gauge was selected for better lateral stability and to allow for higher capacity trains.

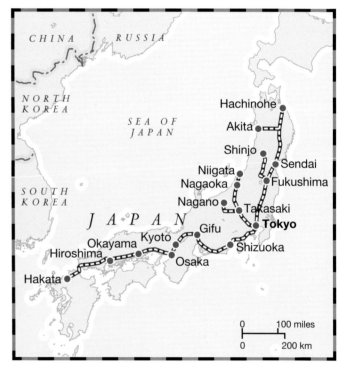

The New Tokaido *Shinkansen* was opened October 1964, so was fully operational in time for the Tokyo World's Fair. The initial 320-mile (515-km) route connected the centre of Tokyo and Osaka with ten intermediate stops. Initial service featured 30 round trips a day running at a maximum speed of 130 mph (209 km/h). The trains were powered by overhead high-voltage AC electric catenary.

The original *Shinkansen* route proved a phenomenal success; it inspired high-speed rail systems around the world and stimulated expansion of the Japanese high-speed network. While the New Tokaido awed observers, JNR's later *Shinkansen* routes were built to even higher standards allowing much faster speeds, while the New Tokaido Line was gradually upgraded.

In the late 1970s and early 1980s, new lines were built north and east of Tokyo. Primary northern routes divide in the Tokyo suburb of Omiya, with the Tohoku Line running due north towards Morioka, while the Joetsu Line aims

Opposite: A Series 400 train approaches the junction at Omiya, north of Tokyo on the Northern Shinkansen. The Series 400 was designed for Tsubasa service from Tokyo to Yamagata, via the Ou line which diverges from the Northern Shinkansen at Fukushima.

northwest towards Niigata. Limited services began in 1982, and additional routes have since been added, while the Tohoku line was extended to Hachinohe and Aomori. Northern *Shinkansen* trains operate from a separate Tokyo terminus. Although cross-platform transfers can be made today from Northern *Shinkansen* Lines to the Tokaido Line at Tokyo Central Station, there is no through-service. There are several reasons for this, first being the assumption that most passengers are destined for Tokyo, Japan's capital and largest city (population 35 million plus). Secondly, since privatization of the JR network in 1987, the lines are operated by different companies. Thirdly, there is a lack of connection between the two networks and operational differences stemming from different voltages used north and south of Tokyo.

Key to *Shinkansen*'s success was a largely tangent route profile despite Japan's predominantly mountainous terrain. This was made possible by extensive tunnelling; the New Sanyo Line (opened between Shin-Osaka and Okayama in 1972) traverses nearly 35 miles (56 km) of tunnel representing more than one third of the line. Northern *Shinkansen* lines also have numerous tunnels: the Joetsu Line is 40 per cent in tunnel, with some stretches being exceptionally long including the famous Daishimizu bore – 13.8 miles (22.2 km) in length.

Further expansion of the Shinkansen network was approved in 2012. Among the most ambitious new routes is development of the new Hokkaido Shinkansen through the existing 33 mile (54 km) under-sea Seikan Tunnel to the northern Island of Hokkaido. This will result in laying dual-gauge track through the tunnel, which opened in 1988. The high speed line is expected to open in 2015; eventually services are planned to connect Sapporo, the island's largest city with Tokyo.

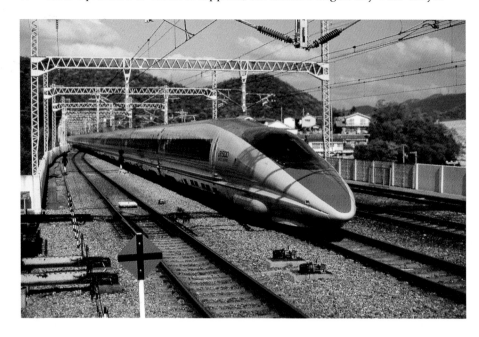

Opposite: *When JR West's Nozomi 500 made its debut in 1997, it was billed as the fastest regularly scheduled train in the world. The train's super sleek profile is necessary to keep sound levels at legal limits when operating at speeds up to 300 mph (480 kph).*

Above: *Series 300 trains were introduced on Nozomi express trains – a premier, extra fare, fast express service – between Tokyo and Hakata. One of these futuristic low-profile trains is seen approaching its Tokyo terminal on the New Tokaido Shinkansen.*

'Bullet' Trains

The original 1964-era 'Series 0' trains, typified by their blue and white bullet noses, were the internationally renowned 'Bullet Trains', and they became iconic symbols of Japanese high-speed rail. These reached the end of their lives many years ago, and would be considered slow by today's standards. Since the 1960s much faster trains were refined, many of which now travel in revenue service at speeds of up to 186 mph (300 km/h), and even faster than that in special test runs. Modern streamlined *Shinkansen* trains are designed with futuristic aerodynamic shapes, and incorporate long tapered noses, wing-like pantographs (electrical collection devices that draw current from overhead catenary), and pantograph shields to minimize the roar of the train sailing along at top speed.

Today, there are eight *Shinkansen* routes, each offering a variety of train services that vary by their exclusivity, price and scheduled speed. Some services use specially designed high-speed trains, while others use more generic *Shinkansen* trains.

On JR Central and JR East routes (on the New Tokaido and New Sanyo Shinkansen routes) *Nozomi* (translates as 'Hope' in English) trains are among the fastest. These premier, extra-fare, extra-fast express services between Tokyo and Hakata call for the most advanced train designs, including the ultra-modern

Below: Series 300 trains embraced an advanced design using an aluminium alloy body with extremely efficient streamlining. This train pauses for a station stop at Kobe.

Series 700 trains noted for their pronounced platypus bill front-end. When the older, but equally futuristic, 500-series trains entered *Nozomi* service in 1997, they were the fastest regularly scheduled trains in the world, and they became virtually an exclusive domain of business executives and the very rich. In early 2013, JR Central introduced its newest high-speed trains; the profoundly futuristic-looking Series-N700A 16 car sets. These are capable of a one-degree body tilt to allow comfortable travel at speeds up to 186 mph (300 km/h) on the New Sanyo Shinkansen.

Above: The Nozomi 500 debuted in March 1997 between Okayama and Hiroshima. Later service was expanded. When this photo was taken the train was travelling faster than half a mile every 10 seconds!

Other modern trains include those for service on Northern *Shinkansen* lines. There are double-deck MAX sets. Also specially designed trains operate off the primary *Shinkansen* network on sinuous routes converted from narrow gauge to standard gauge. Among these are Series 400 trains working the *Tsubasa* ('wings') services between Tokyo to Yamagata and Shinjo (via the Ou line/Yamagata *Shinkansen*) which diverges from the Tohoku Line at Fukushima – 159 miles/ 256 km north of Tokyo Central).

The best way for westerners to experience the Japanese railway network, including high-speed *Shinkansen* routes, is to purchase a Green Pass prior to arrival in Japan. This is valid on most JR trains; however, reservations are required for most *Shinkansen* journeys and further additional fees apply on *Nozomi* trains and in private compartments on high-speed services. The high cost of single tickets for *Shinkansen* trains in Japan can make walk-up travel prohibitively expensive without a pass.

ACROSS JAPAN ON THE OLD NETWORK

Some Narrow-Gauge Highlights

Brian Solomon

Japan was relatively late to adopt railways – its first line wasn't opened until 1872, nearly half a century after the first public railway opened in Britain – yet today it has one of the world's most intensively developed railway systems. Its network measures more than 16,900 miles (27,200 km) in length, of which the vast majority are 3 foot 6 inch (1,067mm) gauge lines, narrow compared to the more common 4 foot 8½ inch (1,435 mm) track gauge used by most American and European railways, and by Japan's famous high-speed *Shinkansen*. While the *Shinkansen* with its futuristic 'bullet trains' symbolizes modern Japanese railways, the *Shinkansen* network is only just over 1,520 miles (2,450 km) long.

Where the *Shinkansen* is a straightforward high-speed double-track line using some of the world's most impressive railway infrastructure for exclusive operation of very fast passenger trains, the rest of the network is a complex system serving every other type of train. Lines range from multiple-track suburban lines around Tokyo to the heavily travelled Tokaido and Chuo mainlines – saturated with a mix of local and express passenger trains as well as freight traffic – and winding single-track lines reaching up into the mountains. Visitors touring Japan are well advised to explore narrow-gauge lines as well as the *Shinkansen*.

Tokyo is laced with narrow-gauge routes. Among the busiest is the famous Yamanote Line or 'Loop' which encircles the city centre with numerous stations. Among the stops are those at Akihabara, an area known for burgeoning discount electronic stores where discriminating shoppers can find the latest high-tech gadgetry, the busy junction at Ueno near one of Tokyo's larger city parks, and

Shinjuku Station which is claimed to be world's busiest with more than 3 million people passing through it on the average weekday. In addition to Yamanote Loop services, the route hosts a variety of other services over portions of the line. While the Loop itself is largely double track, in places the route requires six or more running tracks.

Connecting Tokyo and Osaka is the exceptionally busy traditional Tokaido Line. Saturation on this route in the 1950s encouraged construction of the parallel New Tokaido *Shinkansen* (opened in 1964). Despite the presence of the pioneer high-speed line, the narrow gauge remains one of Japan's most heavily travelled lines. At Fuji – the city named for Japan's famous volcanic mountain and home to Fuji Film – is the junction with the wildly scenic Minobu Line that follows the Fuji River into the mountains. The lower end of the line was opened in 1913, and by 1928 the route was completed stretching over 55 miles (88 km) to the junction with the Chuo Line at Kofu. Today both ends feature regional suburban services, while the central portion of the line has a less frequent service, primarily aimed at line-side mountain resort towns, so much of the route is just single main track, a relatively unusual operating condition in Japan.

Since 1956, in addition to all-stops local trains, the Minobu Line has hosted a fancier run known as the Fujikawa. Eventually this train was granted limited

Above: The luxurious Fujikawa Express glides under a forest of rich spring greenery towards the resort town of Shimobe located deep in a river gorge. The sinuous 3 foot 6 inch (1,067 mm) gauge Minobu Line is largely a single-track route, unusual in Japan where double-track lines are the standard.

express status. Since 1987, when the old Japanese National Railways was broken up into six regional privatized systems, this route has been part of the JR Central network, and in 1995 the Shizouka–Fuji–Kofu *Fujikawa Express* was re-equipped with specially decorated Class 373 EMUs (electric multiple units). These feature large windows and glass ends for better views. The interior is decorated in pastel shades of lavender and burgundy with white and grey accents that mimic the shades of blossoming cherry trees. The best time to ride the line is during April when the cherry flowers are in bloom. There are numerous tunnels and tight curves on the line.

The Chuo Line operated by JR East runs inland east on a sinuous route from Tokyo to Kofu, and then cuts northeasterly to Matsumoto. This route hosts several finely appointed, named streamlined trains including the distinctive *Super Azusa* which since 1993 has used specially styled 12-car E351 trains and works limited express runs over the length of the line, running from Shinjuku Station to Matsumoto in 2 hours and 35 minutes. Since 2001 a train called *The Kaiji*, aimed at business clientele, has worked between Shinjuku and Kofu on an express 100-minute schedule. At Otsuki, the Fuji Kyuko Line diverges from the Chuo Line with local services running to scenic areas with views of Mt Fuji.

Among the fanciest, but least known trains on the Japanese network are the overnight sleeping car trains between major cities. Although these have been in decline in recent years, several runs survive. The poshest is the Tokyo-Ueno to Osaka Cassiopeia which has a 17-hour end-to-end schedule. Other runs include the evocatively named *Twilight Express* from Osaka to Sapporo.

INDIAN PACIFIC

Linking Australia Ocean to Ocean

Colin Nash

The *Indian Pacific* is one of the best-known trains in the world. Stretching from coast to coast across the south of Australia, it first ran in 1970 shortly after the railways of the south of the country were converted to standard gauge. Before that, passengers travelling from Sydney to Perth had to change trains at Broken Hill. The journey is some 2,700 miles (4,345 km) long making it one of the longest train journeys in the world. It takes 65 hours and includes the world's longest stretch of straight railway line: the 296 miles (478 km) across the Nullarbor Plain.

Currently the train runs twice a week in each direction and is operated by Great Southern Rail using Pacific National NR Class diesel locomotives which were introduced in 1997. These locomotives, which have a maximum speed of 70 mph (113 km/h), are the first in Australia to have variable horsepower which makes them the most fuel-efficient in the country. Despite being essentially a luxury train, the *Indian Pacific* is a normally scheduled route. It has three standards of accommodation: premium, first and economy, that are designated as Platinum, Gold Kangaroo and Red Kangaroo. The on-train facilities include the Queen Adelaide Restaurant, serving complimentary meals to first-class passengers, and both single and shared sleeping cars. There are also facilities for carrying cars on double-deck car transporters.

The train departs from East Perth station and travels over the dual-gauge line to Kalgoorlie some 370 miles (595 km) to the east. From there it continues across the treeless waste of the Nullarbor on the old Trans-Australian Railway to the coastal city of Port Augusta, then continues south to Port Pirie before leaving the coast to go inland to Crystal Brook. From Crystal Brook the route heads south to Adelaide, the capital of South Australia. The standard-gauge line from Crystal Brook to Adelaide was opened in 1983 and has added 242 miles (390 km) to the

original route. Prior to 1983 the Indian Pacific did not visit Adelaide due to the gauge disparity that was widespread on Australia's railways. Nowhere is this more apparent than in the historic railway town of Peterborough which sports no less than three rail gauges. On leaving Adelaide the train retraces its route back to Crystal Brook before turning east and passing through Peterborough to head for Broken Hill, then across New South Wales and the Blue Mountains to Sydney's Central Station.

The *Indian Pacific* joins two oceans making it one of the last great coast-to-coast rail journeys in the world. But most of the trip goes through the vast landscape of the Australian continent with all its contrasts. You encounter the splendour of the Blue Mountains and the treeless plains of the Nullarbor; the famous Australian Sun Belt and historic Broken Hill. And from the comfort of the train you can see a fascinating array of wildlife including, if you are very lucky, the Australian wedge tailed eagle with its massive wingspan silhouetted against the clear blue sky. It is this majestic bird that provides the Indian Pacific with its distinctive logo.

In recent years the *Indian Pacific* has run a Christmas Special with notable music personalities onboard. This Special stops at several locations including, in 2005, the remote railway sidings at Watson in the Nullarbor Plain.

Above: *The stylish dining car on the* Indian Pacific.

Right: *A diverted* Indian Pacific *service rounding the curve at Callington at the foot of the Adelaide Hills.*

THE SUNLANDER

Along Australia's Sunshine Coast

Colin Nash

Originally named *The Queenslander*, this was one of the most successful tourist trains running in Australia. It was operated by Queensland Government Railways. Following privatization of the rail network in the 1990s, *The Queenslander* became one of Queensland Rail's services. Under their stewardship the service was renamed *The Sunlander* (after the Sunshine Coast along which the train travels for most of its journey as it connects Brisbane and Cairns) and 'The Queenslander' became the premier class section of that train.

The train is diesel-hauled and sports distinctive silver and blue aluminium coaches. The journey is 1,045 miles (1,682 km) long and is not for those in a hurry as it takes 32 hours to complete. The service has been running for some 50 years and its comfort, high-quality catering and great social atmosphere have made it much admired by holidaymakers and tourists. It is also popular with local train travellers as the train provides a service to towns large and small along the length of the coast including Townsville, the unofficial capital of North Queensland, and Rockhampton, an important transport hub some 370 miles (600 km) north of Brisbane. A full sleeping car service is available in both Standard and Queenslander class, the latter harking back to the original 'Queenslander' heritage and giving that extra touch of luxury by offering traditional all-inclusive service. The private compartments, gourmet dining, entertainment, personalized service and local commentary make it a veritable hotel on rails.

The route runs three times a week in each direction. It is a relaxing, comfortable journey as the train takes passengers from the state capital to the tropical climate of Cairns where the Great Barrier Reef meets the timeless Daintree Rainforest wilderness. For the numerous holidaymakers who use the train, the superb ever-

Opposite: The Sunlander in the lush Queensland countryside.

changing scenery slipping by the window as it snakes its way along the coast is undoubtedly a highlight of the journey. This includes the Glasshouse Mountains, volcanic crags discovered by Captain Cook which are about 50 minutes out of Nambour Station; cane fields around Bundaberg and Mackay and along the coast north of Townsville; and lush rainforest at the northern end of the journey.

Many tour operators make use of the 'Queenslander' facilities onboard *The Sunlander* as an essential part of their itinerary and it has been chosen as one of the World's Top 25 Rail Journeys by the Society of International Railway Travellers.

The intention is that by the middle of 2014 *The Sunlander* service will be run by newly refurbished and upgraded tilting trains, including one completely new set, following an investment of A$189 million by the Queensland government. These trains will run at speeds of up to 100 mph (161 km/h) and will cut five hours from the journey time while retaining and improving on the existing, much appreciated onboard service. The old 'Queenslander' stock is due to be decommissioned after 45 years of service.

Above: Artist's impression of the modern airy restaurant car in the upgraded Sunlander *due to enter service in 2014.*

Above left: The Sunlander *passing through cane fields as it nears Bundaberg.*

Opposite: The Sunlander *leaving Bundaberg for Brisbane.*

TRANZALPINE

New Zealand's Great Day Out

Colin Nash

The *TranzAlpine* runs daily in each direction between Christchurch, the second largest city in South Island, and Greymouth. It is widely regarded as one of the most scenic train trips in the world. The journey is 139 miles (224 km) long and takes four and a half hours as the train crosses South Island from coast to coast. It is possible to do the return journey in a day with a brief stay at the destination, making it a popular and picturesque day out.

The train is currently operated by the KiwiRail Scenic Journeys subsidiary of Kiwi Rail, a state-owned enterprise founded in 2008 as the railways operations subsidiary of New Zealand Railways Corporation: the latest in a long line of companies operating rail services in New Zealand, both private and public and dating back to the 19th century. The line is 3 feet 6 inches (1,067 mm) in gauge and trains use diesel traction, typically the General Motors DC Class. These locomotives were originally the 85-strong Canadian-built DA Class that were found in both Australia and New Zealand, but on being rebuilt locally they were re-named DC. They have a top speed of 56–62 mph (90–100 km/h). New Zealand AK class cars, built in Dunedin's Hillside Workshops especially for KiwiRail's scenic routes, entered service in 2013.

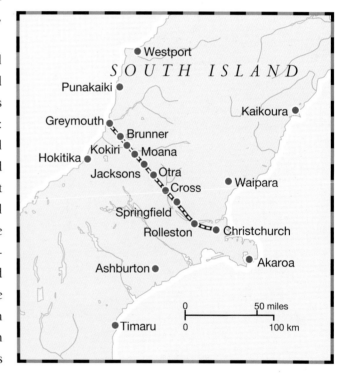

On leaving Christchurch the train passes through lush farmland, fields of sheep, cattle and red deer and the small town of Darfield before entering the foothills of the Southern Alps. Once into the mountains, the train crosses a series of steel girder bridges over deep gorges and over the famous 'Staircase' viaduct which soars 240 feet (73 m) above the river and has spectacular views. Beyond the Staircase the hills give way to mountains, their peaks shrouded in mist.

Midway through the journey the train stops at Arthur's Pass surrounded by more mist-laden peaks before plunging into the 5.3-mile (8.6-km) long Otira

Opposite: A pair of Kiwi Rail's General Motors diesel-electric locomotives leads a passenger train west of Arthur's Pass. The railway passes dramatic scenery made famous by the Lord of the Rings films.

Tunnel which is one of the longest in New Zealand. The tunnel was originally electrified because the build-up of fumes in its steeply graded shaft made it unsuitable for the steam-powered trains of the day. However, the electric system was discontinued in 1997. The tunnel still requires additional ventilation to combat diesel fumes from the locomotives and because of this the open-air viewing car on the *TranzAlpine* is closed during its time in the tunnel.

The journey continues along a deep river valley flanked by misty mountains. The train criss-crosses the river, with its numerous waterfalls, on a series of bridges, which, together with the tranquillity of Lake Brunner in the west coast area (about half an hour from Greymouth), make this a particularly impressive part of the journey. As the train approaches Greymouth it passes the Old Brunner Mine with its suspension bridge linking the railway with the site of the mine. In 1896 this was the scene of New Zealand's worst coal mining disaster. Greymouth itself is a small town but nevertheless is the west coast's main centre. The *TranzAlpine* stays in Greymouth for only an hour before starting its return journey, so day trippers just have time to grab some quick refreshment. But the town is also an interchange for bus services to destinations down the west coast and is a great base for visits to the ever popular glaciers and to Punakaiki, on the edge of the Paparoa National Park, with its spectacular Pancake Rocks and Blowholes.

Above: Trains on the TranzAlpine run crest at Arthur's Pass 2,418 feet (737 m) above sea level. Arthur's Pass National Park is a popular layover point, where towering peaks reach 6,560 feet (2,000 m) into the sky. An excursion train is seen east of the pass. The AK class cars have large panoramic windows and run on newly designed, air-cushioned P11 bogies.

Opposite above: Among the scenic highlights of the ascent of Arthur's Pass is the confluence of Bealey and Mingha Rivers.

Opposite below: Kiwi Rail diesels lead a train across the famed Staircase Viaduct, the highest bridge on the TranzAlpine route which spans its namesake Staircase Gully.

RESOURCES

Bibliography

Die Güterbahnen (*Freight Railways*). Düsseldorf: Verband Deutscher Verkehrsunternehmen, 2002.

Albi, Charles, and Kenton Forrest. *The Moffat Tunnel, A Brief History*. Golden, Colo.: Colorado Railroad Museum, 1984.

Allen, G. Freeman. *The Fastest Trains in the World*. London: Scribners, 1978.

Allen, Geoffrey Freeman. *Modern Railways*. London: Hamlyn, 1980.

Beller, Steven. *A Concise History of Austria*. Cambridge University Press, 2006.

Binney, Marcus, and David Pearce, eds. *Railway Architecture*. London: Bloomsbury Books, 1979.

Boyd, J.I.C. *The Ffestiniog Railway, Vols. 1 & 2*. England, 1975.

Burgess, George, H., and Miles C. Kennedy, *Centennial History of the Pennsylvania Railroad*. Philadelphia: Pennsylvania Railroad Company, 1949.

Butcher, Alan C. *Railways Restored 2004*. Hersham, Surray, UK: Ian Allen Publishing, 2004.

Conrad, Ernst. *Bernina Express*. München, Germany: 1986.

Crump, Spencer. *Riding the Cumbres & Toltec Scenic Railroad*. Corona del Mar, Calif., 1992.

Cupper, Dan. *Horseshoe Heritage, The Story of a Great Railroad Landmark*. Halifax, Pa.: Horseshoe Curve National Historic Landmark, 1996.

Dodson, Rob. *Eastern Europe by Rail*. Chalfont St. Peter, Bucks, England: Bradt Publications; Old Saybrook, Conn. : Globe Pequot Press, 1994.

Doherty, Timothy Scott, and Brian Solomon. *Conrail*. St. Paul, Minn., 2004.

Dover, A. T. *Electric Traction – A Treatise on the Application of Electric Power to Tramways and Railways*. London: Sir Isaac Pitman & Sons, Ltd., 1925.

Drury, George H. *The Historical Guide to North American Railroads*. Waukesha, Wis., 1985.

Dubin, Arthur D. *Some Classic Trains*. Milwaukee, Wisconsin. 1964.

More Classic Trains. Milwaukee, Wisconsin: Kalmbach Publishing Co., 1974.

Ellis, Hamilton. *British Railway History* 1830-1876. London: George Allen and Urwin Ltd., 1954

Ellis, Hamilton. *The Pictorial Encyclopedia of Railways*. London: Hamlyn, 1968.

Fox, Peter, and Robert Pritchard. *Preserved Locomotives of British Railways*. Sheffield, UK; Platform 5 Publishing, 2009.

Harlow, Alvin F. *Steelways of New England*. New York: Creative Age Press, 1946.

Harris, Ken, ed. *World Electric Locomotives*. London: Ny Jane's 1981, 1981.

Hendry, R. Powell. *Narrow Gauge Story*. Rugby, England, 1979.

Hilton, George W. *American Narrow Gauge Railroads*. Stanford, Calif., 1990.

Hogg, Garry Lester. *Orient Express – The birth, life and death of a great train*. London: Hutchinson, 1968

Jackson, Alan, A. *London's Termini*. Newton Abbot: 1969.

Jones, Mervyn. *The Essential Guide to Austrian Railways and Tramways*. Usk, Mon, UK: The Oakwood Press, 2008.

Kann, Robert A. *A History of the Habsburg Empire 1526–1918*. Berkeley and Los Angeles: Unversity of California Press, 1974.

Lamb, W. Kaye. *History of the Canadian Pacific Railway*. New York: Macmillan Co., 1977.

Lambert, Anthony J. *Heritage Railways of the British Isles*. London: Grange, 1999.

Marshall, John. *The Guinness Book of Rail Facts and Feats*. Enfield, Middlesex, United Kingdom: Guinness Superlatives, 1975.

Meeks, Carroll L. V. *The Railroad Station*. New Haven, CT: Yale Univ. Press, 1956.

Middleton, William D. *When the Steam Railroads Electrified*. Milwaukee, 1974.

Grand Central . . . the World's Greatest Railway Terminal. San Marino, CA: Golden West Books.1977.

Metropolitan Railways – Rapid Transit in North America. Indiana University Press. Bloomington, Indiana, 2003.

Middleton, William D. with George M. Smerk, and Roberta L. Diehl. *Encyclopedia of North American Railroads*. Indiana University Press, Bloomington and Indianapolis, 2007.

Morgan, Bryan. *The Railway-Lover's Companion*. London: Eyre and Spottiswoode Ltd, 1963.

Osterwald, Doris B. *Cinders & Smoke*. Lakewood, Colo. 1995.

Osterwald, Doris B. *Ticket to Toltec*. Denver, 1992.

Potter, Janet Greenstein. *Great American Railroad Stations*. New York: Preservation Press, 1996.

Protheroe, Ernest. *The Railways of the World*. London: George Routledge & Sons, no date.

Pratt, Edwin A. *American Railways*. Macmillan and Co., London, 1903.

Pratt, Edwin A. *Railways and Nationalization*. P.S. King & Son., London, 1908.

Ransome, P.T.J. *Narrow Gauge Steam*. Oxford, 1996.

Ransome-Wallis, P. *World Railway Locomotives*. New York: Hawthorn, 1959.

Roberts, Charles S., and Gary W. Schlerf. *Triumph I – Altoona to Pitcairn 1846–1996*. Bernard, Roberts and Co., Baltimore, Maryland, 1997.

Ross, David. *The Encyclopedia of Trains & Locomotives*. San Diego, Calif.,: Thunder Bay Press, 2007.

Semmens, P.W.B. *High Speed in Japan*. Sheffield, United Kingdom: 1997.

Simmons, Jack. *Rail 150, The Stockton & Darlington Railway and What Followed*. London: Eyre Methuen, 1975.

Snell, J. B. *Early Railways*. London, 1972.

Solomon, Brian, *Alco Locomotives*. Minneapolis, Minn.: Voyageur Press, 2009.

The American Diesel Locomotive. St. Paul, Minn.: MBI Publishing Co. 2000.

Amtrak. St. Paul, Minn.: MBI Publishing Company, 2005

Bullet Trains. Osceola, WI: MBI Publishing, 2001.

Burlington Northern Santa Fe Railway. St. Paul, Minn.: MBI Publishing Company, 2005.

CSX. St. Paul, Minn.: MBI Publishing Company, 2005.

EMD Locomotives. St. Paul, Minn.: MBI Publishing Company, 2006.

Railroads of California. Voyageur Press. Minneapolis, MN, 2009.

Railroads of Pennsylvania. Voyageur Press. Minneapolis, MN, 2008.

Railway Masterpieces: Celebrating the World's Greatest Trains, Stations and Feats of Engineering. Iola, Wis.: Krause Publishing, 2002.

Southern Pacific Railroad. Osceola, Wis.: MBI Publishing Company, 1999.

Trains of the Old West. New York: Michael Friedman Publishing Group, 1998.

Stilgoe, John R. *Metropolitan Corridor*. New Haven, CT: Yale Univ. Press, 1983.

Stretton, Clement E. *The Development of the Locomotive – A Popular History 1803–1896*. London: Bracken Books, 1989.

Talbot, F. A. *Railway Wonders of the World, Volumes 1 & 2*. London: Cassell & Co., 1914.

Taplin, Michael and Michael Russell. *Trams in Eastern Europe*. Harrow Weald, Middlesex, UK: Capital Transport Publishing, 2003.

Taylor, Arthur. *Hi-Tech Trains*. London: Apple Press, 1992.

Whitelegg, John and Staffan Hultén. *High Speed Trains: Fast Tracks to the Future*. Burtersett, Hawes, North Yorkshire, UK: Leading Edge Press and Publishing, 1993.

Winchester, Clarence. *Railway Wonders of the World, Volumes 1 & 2*. London:1935.

Periodicals

Jane's World Railways, London.

Journal of the Irish Railway Record Society, Dublin, Ireland.

Official Guide to the Railways, New York

RailNews, Waukesha, Wis. [no longer published]

Railroad History (*formerly Railway and Locomotive Historical Society Bulletin*), Boston, Mass.

The Railway Gazette, London.

Thomas Cook, European Timetable.

Today's Railways. Sheffield, United Kingdom.

TRAINS, Waukesha, Wis.

Web Resources

english.jr-central.co.jp English language site on Japan's JR Central operations and news.

reiseauskunft.bahn.de DB Bahn's schedules site provides excellent European timetable information.

www.amtrakcalifornia.com Official Amtrak California website for timetables, station information, routes, and special low fares.

www.amtrak.com Amtrak's website for timetables, maps, and reservations.

www.conwayscenic.com Official Conway Scenic Railroad site.

www.cumbrestoltec.com Official Cumbres & Toltec Scenic Railroad site.

www.ferromex.com.mx and *www.ferromex.com.mx/turis/chepe.html* Spanish language site on Ferromax operations in Mexico.

www.festrail.co.uk Official site for Ffestiniog and Welsh Highland Railways.

www.hsb-wr.de Official Harzer Schmalspur Bahnen website with schedules, events, and details of Harz mountain railway operations.

www.jreast.co.jp Official JR East website with information on Shinkansen and other lines east of Toyko.

www.maineeasternrailroad.com Official Maine Eastern Railroad site

www.nationalrail.co.uk Official site for timetable information in the United Kingdom.

www.rail.co.uk Provides details on railway travel planning in the United Kingdom.

www.renfe.com Spanish language site, official website for RENFE, operators of the AVE high-speed train services.

www.rhb.ch Official Rhätische Bahn website with details on Bernina and Glacier Express, schedules, maps, and other information.

www.settle-carlisle.co.uk Website for the Settle & Carlisle Partnership, features schedules, guides, news, and history about the S&C route.

www.svr.co.uk Official Severn Valley Railway website, with schedules, history, events, and information about stations and equipment.

www.viarail.ca Official VIA Rail site.

www.zugspitze.de Official Zugspitzbahn site.

INDEX

This edition first published in the United Kingdom in 2013 by
John Beaufoy Publishing,
11 Blenheim Court, 316 Woodstock Road, Oxford OX2 7NS, England
www.johnbeaufoy.com

10 9 8 7 6 5 4 3 2 1

ISBN 978-1-909612-05-1

Edited, designed and typeset by Stonecastle Graphics
Cartography by William Smuts
Project management by Rosemary Wilkinson

Printed and bound in Malaysia by Times Offset (M) Sdn. Bhd.